UNCOMMON SENSE

UNCOMMON SENSE

EMBRACE THE STRUGGLE TO SUCCEED

ROBERT M DONOVAN, MBA

Uncommon Sense: Embrace the Struggle to Succeed
Copyright © 2024 by Rob M. Donovan, MBA

Requests for information should be sent to: Rob.donovangroup@gmail.com at Donovan Development, Inc. Visit Donovandevelopment.com.

Any internet addresses (websites, blogs, etc.) in this book are offered as a resource. They are not intended in any way to be or imply an endorsement by Donovan Development, Inc., nor does Donovan Development, Inc. vouch for the content of these sites and contact numbers for the life of this book.

All rights reserved. No part of this book, including icons and images, may be reproduced in any manner without prior written permission from the copyright holder, except where noted in the text and in the case of brief quotations embodied in critical articles and reviews.

All Scripture quotations, unless otherwise indicated, are taken from the Holy Bible, New International Version®, NIV®. Copyright © 1973, 1978, 1984, 2011 by Biblica, Inc.® Used by permission of Zondervan. All rights reserved worldwide. www.zondervan.com. The "NIV" and "New International Version" are trademarks registered in the United States Patent and Trademark Office by Biblica, Inc.®

Scripture quotations marked (AMP) are taken from the Amplified® Bible (AMP), Copyright © 2015 by The Lockman Foundation. Used by permission. lockman.org.

Scripture quotations marked (ESV) are taken from the ESV® Bible (The Holy Bible, English Standard Version®). Copyright © 2001 by Crossway, a publishing ministry of Good News Publishers. Used by permission. All rights reserved.

Scripture quotations marked (NLT) are taken from the Holy Bible, New Living Translation. Copyright © 1996, 2004, 2015 by Tyndale House Foundation. Used by permission of Tyndale House Ministries, Carol Stream, Illinois 60188. All rights reserved.

Scripture quotations marked (NASB) are taken from the (NASB®) New American Standard Bible®, Copyright © 1960, 1971, 1977, 1995 by The Lockman Foundation. Used by permission. All rights reserved. lockman.org.

Scripture quotations marked (KJV) are taken from the Holy Bible, King James Version (Authorized Version).

Scripture marked (NKJV) are taken from the New King James Version®. Copyright © 1982 by Thomas Nelson, Inc. Used by permission. All rights reserved.

Scripture quotations marked (TLB) are taken from The Living Bible copyright © 1971. Used by permission of Tyndale House Publishers, a Division of Tyndale House Ministries, Carol Stream, Illinois 60188. All rights reserved.

All emphases in Scripture quotations and other quotations are the author's. Capitalization has occasionally been modified from the original.

ISBN 979-8-9866242-3-5 (Paperback); ISBN 979-8-9866242-5-9 (Kindle);
ISBN 979-8-9866242-4-2 (ePub)

TABLE OF CONTENTS

Introduction 1
CHAPTER 1.   The Grind. 5
CHAPTER 2.   Planning 23
CHAPTER 3.   Action vs. Movement 31
CHAPTER 4.   Leadership 41
CHAPTER 5.   The Great I AM 49
CHAPTER 6.   B.B.B. (Building Business Biblically) 53
CHAPTER 7.   Embrace the Suck 69
CHAPTER 8.   There Is No Such Thing as a Short-Term Plan . . 85
CHAPTER 9.   Giving 89
CHAPTER 10. Go with Your Gut (Decision-Making) 95
CHAPTER 11. Cash Flow 101
CHAPTER 12. Debt 115
CHAPTER 13. Monday Quarterback 119
CHAPTER 14. Keeping Up vs. Catching Up 125
CHAPTER 15. Practice 133
CHAPTER 16. Self-Made 139
CHAPTER 17. Newton's Law 149
CHAPTER 18. Feeding the Ego 153
CHAPTER 19. Closing Thoughts 163
About the Author 167

INTRODUCTION

This book is dedicated to my family. Without them by my side, I wouldn't be the man that I am. Having them in my corner supporting and helping me with the words you read and standing behind me helps me live the life and do the things that I teach in this book. This book is a summary of all the "What-did-you-do-today?" questions from my kids as I got home from work. Instead of summarizing and giving them a generic answer, I decided to dive deep into what I actually do and how I live my life in hopes of teaching them and showing them how we can use our gifts that God has blessed us with to help others.

My ministry is to teach Biblical principles of business and finance to all. My hope is that we will have a society that turns to God and the Bible for their questions rather than social media and salespeople who profit from their decisions. I thank you for spending your precious time and money to read this book, and if you enjoyed it, please pass it on to someone else, too. As with all my books, 100 percent of the profit is donated to our missions partners with the purpose of spreading the Word of God around the world and helping those in need through outreach programs. If you are a church, school, or a not-for-profit and would like resources for group or classroom settings, please contact us at www.donovandevelopment.com.

God laid it on my heart to put together a Biblically based book to help entrepreneurs just like myself set up and build their businesses under Biblical principles. This guidance is not typically taught in traditional books and business schools and has been lost from the society we step out into and operate in every day. These principles are simple. As a basis of understanding, every decision we make comes from the Bible.

In action, though, this can become a complex concept when we are faced with everyday problems and the norms of planning, building, and running our companies. What I have found while developing my own business plans and consulting for others is that the foundation of the plan—the core piece—has to be centered on one thing and one thing only. Once we have this core, then all our decisions come down to just falling into line with our core belief. This is our building block. Our non-negotiable. Our foundation. Our decisions become black and white. They become right and wrong. They become as clear to us as left and right.

This core belief is short and sweet, it's simple, and it can stand the test of time. It holds the promise for your life. Now, all you have to do is just let yourself believe, follow it wholeheartedly, and hold steadfastly to the teachings. This core belief is that the Bible is the living, breathing Word of God. The core belief is that if God said it, then it's true. If

He said it before, then it is still true today. The promises and truths in the Bible are alive and can bring new life to any business at any stage.

> Faith is the assurance (title deed, confirmation) of things hoped for (divinely guaranteed), and the evidence of things not seen [the conviction of their reality—faith comprehends as fact what cannot be experienced by the physical senses]. (Hebrews 11:1 AMP)

If you believe that the Bible is the living, breathing Word of God, then the words spoken through Scripture lay out a perfect plan—a road map—to develop and implement a perfectly matched plan laid out on earth as it is in heaven through the promises and teachings of God to us all. Through this book, I will lay out step-by-step instructions to help your business at any stage. It doesn't matter if you are sitting at home praying for an opportunity to come your way, or if you're a seasoned entrepreneur looking to expand, grow, or start a new or additional business. I will show you how to develop a business that not only gives glory and honor to God but is also a blessing to you. With God, all things are possible. "Jesus looked at them and said, 'With man this is impossible, but with God all things are possible.'"

CHAPTER 1

THE GRIND

Looking back, we can see that every great business throughout history has had an incredible leader—an owner with a true passion. One that wasn't afraid of taking risks, thinking outside the box, or stepping out to take on a competitor or industry in the face of what appeared to be certain failure. These great leaders were able to accomplish so much and to build legacies for themselves and their families throughout history. They were also able to leave their mark on this world through the real objectives they had in mind. When we think about these accomplishments and the determination that was needed to see these visions through, it truly is awe-inspiring. There is no doubt that these names become synonymous with the businesses they created. Henry Ford and the automobile, Rockefeller and Standard Oil, Carnegie and the steel industry, Steve Jobs and Apple, Bill Gates and Microsoft, Elon Musk and Tesla. These are just some of the household names whose products defined or created industries to change the world.

When I first started out back in 2005, I dreamt of one day making a similar mark on the world—building a business that stood the test of time and brought me fame and fortune along the way. But you see, what I didn't have when I set out all those years ago was a plan. My plan was simple in theory—I wanted to develop a turnkey real estate, mortgage, and construction company that offered a one-stop shop for all your real estate, development, remodeling, and financing needs. In theory it was simple. These companies would run independently but also share the same back office to help cut costs and to improve efficiencies for data and interoffice bookkeeping and scheduling.

The crossover design allowed the same staff to be used for multifaceted purposes, and as I rolled out my vision, we saw immediate success across all product lines. We were building a real estate portfolio while helping buyers and sellers buy and sell homes. These same buyers were using our mortgage services to secure funding for their real estate transactions, and the mortgage company was providing financing to these same customers for their remodeling projects. We experienced unprecedented growth and in 2007 purchased and moved our operations into a new office space.

What we didn't expect were the extreme challenges that 2007 and 2008 would bring to us that really brought forth the turning point from what I will call business plan 1.0 to business plan 2.0. In 2007–2008, most of the United States went through what has been called the worst real estate market collapse in history. Home prices collapsed 12.4 percent in the fourth quarter of 2008. Mortgage foreclosures and short sales increased to 45 percent of all home sales.[1] New home construction came to a halt, falling 27.2 percent in 2008.[2] I had a plan, I had the vision, I had the goal, and I implemented this new plan in real-world application, but three years after formation, I was staring at a whole new set of problems that I hadn't prepared for. We had foreclosure levels at an all-time high. People couldn't pay their mortgages. Homes were being taken back by banks. No one wanted to remodel these homes.

The mortgage industry rewrote the narrative what seemed like overnight. Lenders and banks were declaring bankruptcy every day from these mortgage-backed securities that were developed as safe, and diversified investments ended up being time bombs for their lenders and investors. Some of the biggest financial institutions—Lehman Brothers, Bear Sterns, IndyMac, and even Washington Mutual, which was the largest bank failure in the history of the FDIC[3]—were tumbling to the ground. Mortgage companies, banks, and lenders were operating one day, and employees would show up the next day to locked doors.

From the outside looking in, it looked as if my fledgling company had no chance for survival. Our lenders were drying up, and the ones that were still around were changing the rules of the game on a day-to-day basis. No one wanted to lend money anymore. The fear of default and foreclosure was catastrophic. We were faced with some serious

---

1. Les Christie, "Home Prices in Record Plunge," CNN Money, February 12, 2009, money.cnn.com/2009/02/12/real_estate/Latest_median_prices/.

2. "Construction Spending Drops by Record in 2008," NBC News, February 2, 2009, nbcnews.com/news/amp/wbna28977216.

3. "Status of Washington Mutual Bank Receivership," FDIC, October 23, 2020, accessed December 1, 2023, fdic.gov/resources/resolutions/bank-failures/failed-bank-list/wamu-settlement.html.

decisions—decisions that I wasn't equipped for. I had no experience in navigating these times. These were the same waters that were taking down institutions that had been around for hundreds of years. Determined not to give up, we were forced to change direction.

In January 2009, we officially shut the doors on our mortgage company. In life, when you get dealt a bad hand or things don't go as planned, there are really only two things that you can do. The first is to complain, say how it's not fair, have a pity party, and then give up. As a business owner, especially when first starting out, I remember having these temper tantrums probably once a week. The second option that you have is to dust yourself off, pick yourself up off the ground, and keep going. Our mortgage company had been hemorrhaging, and our construction and real estate companies were barely staying afloat. The little each was generating was barely keeping the others above water. We had to make a decision and we had to make it fast. We had newly unemployed employees from our mortgage company, and we had this newly purchased office space—we just didn't have a product or service for them anymore.

Call it faith, call it dumb luck, call it right place at the right time. My partner got a call from an old friend. During their conversation, my partner explained how we had to shut the mortgage business down, how we now were faced with what to do with these employees, and how things weren't looking promising. At that moment, we were having our own pity party. "What did we do to deserve this?" But that one call opened the door of opportunity that we easily could have overlooked. In the conversation, this friend asked if we'd ever heard of an up-and-coming tax-preparation franchise that was looking to expand. Florida (where our main office was located) was available. "Would you be interested in opening and developing this new tax franchise?" he asked. We looked at each other, took about fifteen seconds to think about the answer, and said, "Yes, what do you need from us?"

Now, logically thinking through, this was not a no-brainer. We had no tax-preparation knowledge, we had no experience, we had no background in this product or industry, and we didn't have employees that were capable (and we hadn't even talked to them to see if they were willing to make this transition). But what we did have was confidence in our own abilities and in the fact that we would rather be up to bat and trying something than sitting on the bench doing nothing.

The excitement lasted for about three minutes, and then the realization sank in. We now had to come up with half of the franchise fee to even get the opportunity to take this at bat. Just another day in the life of an entrepreneur. Somehow, we were able to pull it all together, and in January of 2009, we transitioned from a mortgage company to a full-service tax-prep company in the course of eleven days, which just so happened to be how many days we had until tax filing officially opened with the IRS. This was a whirlwind for sure. It was all hands on deck, and all ideas were good ideas. Remember, we had no idea what we were doing, so we had no reference point on if they were actual good ideas or bad ideas—but they were ideas, and we were committed.

Business cards—check, signage—check, letterhead—check, training manual—check, training resources—check, software—check, employee training—check. The list seemed never-ending. We were working sixteen- to twenty-hour days either at the office, remodeling, setting up the new business, or doing tax training, all while still keeping the real estate and construction businesses up and running to help support this new venture until it could get off its feet. We were burning the candle at both ends, and that was just to get us into tax season. Now the real work was about to begin.

The day finally came, and we were now officially a tax franchise. Was our newfound business and investment going to pay off? Could we profitably transition our plan from 1.0 to 2.0? Would anyone trust us to work with them? What in the world did we get ourselves into? All these questions raced through my mind the first day tax filing opened. We had done all we could possibly do up to that point. So, all we could do now was execute on all the hard work and keep the hammer down on marketing and advertising through tax season to see how it all paid off. There is a famous adage about a Kirby vacuum salesman that used to sell vacuums door to door. With each *no*, his excitement grew because he knew that each *no* meant that he was getting that much closer to a *yes*.

Here is a summary of our first week of tax season:
- Day 1: 0 customers
- Day 2: 0 customers
- Day 3: 0 customers
- Day 4: 0 customers
- Day 5: 0 customers
- Day 6: 0 customers
- Day 7: 2 customers

The Grind

The total count in week one of our new tax-prep business was two customers. Now, in business you have to take risks. You have to have courage. You have to have the ability to persevere. But two customers over a seven-day timeframe, with our offices open seven days a week twelve hours per day Monday through Saturday and six hours on Sunday, we were talking seventy-eight hours of being in the office for two returns at thirty-nine hours of work per return. We were not in a good place financially, but we were not going to give up. We stuck it out through the tax season, and we ended up with 139 total returns filed through our new tax-preparation office. With a lot of blood, sweat, and tears, we ended up breaking even for our first tax season (not including our investment in the tax franchise), and corporate was impressed with our performance (they hadn't had much faith in us making it through, we later found out). They invited us to come meet with them along with some of the other franchise owners.

When first arriving and sitting in on the year-end recap meeting, I remember staring dumbfounded at how it was possible that we had made it through without any of the support, resources, and tools available. Short of the online training that we took and had our brokers take, we did it all *our way*. Aka *the hard way*. It was like seeing fire for the first time. All those twenty-plus-hour days recreating the wheel just to create a square equivalent were mind-blowing.

After the meeting, we got to meet with the founder and CEO. He asked us about our first season, and we told him all the stories and pitfalls. We all got a few chuckles, but the key takeaway ended up being that if we could do what we did with no help, then we must have something in us. We left that meeting with a new sense of excitement, along with the development rights for the state of Florida. What this meant was that if anyone wanted to open a new franchise in the state, they would contact us, and we would walk them through the process and support them with their new business. With this, we also had the right to open up new locations in areas that didn't have any current franchises so that we could spread the name of the company and increase our business at the same time. This was truly an amazing opportunity and gave us something to work on during the offseason while we set up, prepped, and got ready for next year's tax season.

As the 2009 tax season got rolling (that is, in 2010), we hit the ground running. We ended our first development season bringing on four new franchise owners in Florida, we opened a second brick-and-mortar location in our local market, and we purchased an existing CPA business in Jacksonville, Florida, which we transitioned to the franchise model to give us a third brick-and-mortar location. In addition to these locations, we partnered with a check-cashing business to allow us to set up onsite kiosks in their stores for the tax season. From our one location in 2009, we ended up with eight tax-prep locations across the state of Florida. We were finally starting to catch our groove, and for our second tax season, we were able to prepare 1,112 tax returns, making us profitable in our second year in the business.

Our real estate business was continuing to acquire properties, and our construction company continued to survive through the downturn of the real estate market without any pitfalls. We realized that the foreclosure market presented an opportunity for both our real estate and our construction businesses. Most of these foreclosure properties were "distressed," meaning they were in need of work. Who better to do the work than our construction company? By tweaking our business plan to not only buy distressed properties but also cater to investors looking to purchase these distressed properties that needed a contractor to do the work, we were able to survive and thrive through the 2007–2010 downturn of the real estate market.

Entering our third tax season in 2011, we had high hopes. We had another successful development year, bringing on four more franchisees, and we once again expanded our own reach with four additional kiosks in Northeast Florida as well as seven in South Florida. We entered the next tax season with nineteen locations ready and able to service tax needs. This could have been our breakout year—we had the infrastructure, the experience, the support staff, and the brick-and-mortar locations to make it all possible.

Tax season opened, and we were off to the races. All our locations were firing on all cylinders. Then the unthinkable happened. First Republic Bank, the bank that funded the rapid-refund loans for our customers, ceased doing business with corporate. Overnight, we once again had the rug pulled out from under us, and the writing was once again on the wall that we were about to face a rough landing. Just like that, we lost the ability to conduct 85 percent of our business. We had no product, and we were now at the same crossroads that the mortgage industry had brought us to just two short years prior. In effect, we were Chick-fil-A without the ability to sell a chicken sandwich.

We consolidated locations and searched endlessly for other products and lenders that would take over where First

Republic left off, to no avail. Facing another collapse outside of our control, we had no choice but to wind down our current operations.[4]

To say that this was a time of extreme stress is an understatement. We had invested so much time, money, effort, and resources into this season that we were really on the edge of physical and mental breakdown. My wife and I were engaged, with our wedding date scheduled for April 16, the day after tax season ended, which just added to the to-do list, stress, and emotions as that day got closer and closer. Couple a second failed business in three years with the fact that I'm about to get married—plus I'm once again barely keeping things afloat with the real estate and construction company.

But for some reason, this time felt different. My wife and I had started going to church in the spring of 2009, and this was the first time in my life that I had been exposed to church and the Biblical teachings of Jesus Christ. I was in the infancy of my walk with Christ, but while on the outside I was dealing with and going through all this extreme stress, I had a sense of calmness and peace inside of me.

When we talk about this story, it's amazing because it almost didn't happen. It's true in the Bible as in life that God speaks to people. He comes to some in a burning bush, some He speaks to directly, to some He comes in a vision or through angels, etc. But to most, He comes in a whisper. A

---

4. It was later discovered that the CEO of this company was indicted and sentenced to jail for conspiring to commit fraud. Through this indictment, we also found out that corporate didn't have a relationship with First Republic for the 2011 tax season to offer the products they had told us as franchise owners we had to support our customers. "Founder of Nationwide Tax Return Company Sentenced to Prison for Fraud and Tax Crimes," Office of Public Affairs, Department of Justice, January 10, 2022, accessed December 1, 2023, justice.gov/opa/pr/founder-nationwide-tax-return-preparation-company-sentenced-prison-fraud-and-tax-crimes.

whisper woke me up in the middle of the night—a whisper that when I woke in the morning I shrugged off as a stupid idea that made no sense. Was it a dream? Was it another crazy idea like I had had so many times in the past? This was a whisper that I could have easily shrugged off and ignored and gone about my day. But nonetheless, the whisper was there.

As I walked into the office that morning, my partner was sitting at his desk, stressed out and anxious. He had been applying for jobs and was now deliberating moving himself and his family halfway across the country, having just accepted a job doing sales for a company that he didn't want to work for but needed to support his family. Decisions in life sometimes don't come down to what you want. We had been doing what we wanted for the last four years, and the results were two failed businesses for our work. But the circumstances necessitated the change, and moving cross-country seemed to be the only reasonable decision he could make for the betterment and support of his family.

I remember this day like it was yesterday. It was Monday, April 4, 2011, and I came into the office just like every other morning. But this morning was different. In passing—and thinking back in retrospect, almost under my breath because I knew my partner had already made a decision to move and had accepted a new job—I said, "Do you want to start a roofing company?" I remember a half chuckle and then the words that would change the narrative for things to come. "How many leads can you get?"

Now the backstory for this is that in 2008–2009, when things were slowing down, I had obtained a roofing license to allow the construction company to take on more work and give us the opportunity to do more projects and larger scopes of work to get us through. At that time, we were doing lots of foreclosure rehab, and with that came the need for new roofs on our projects. It was never my intention to start a roofing company—I was just looking for a way to keep the construction company open, trying to stay ahead of the game to make sure the doors stayed open and everyone stayed employed.

The whisper now had ignited something in my partner's eyes. I responded to his question: "I'm not 100 percent sure, but I'm guessing twenty to thirty a month." Just like the fifteen-second decision that we made when we got the call about the tax-franchise opportunity, another fifteen-second conversation turned into another all-hands-on-deck decision to go after it. The next call was to the marketing company that we were using to help provide us with leads for the construction company. (Spoiler alert—fast forward ten years, and this same company would purchase our roofing business.)

We confirmed that they would be able to provide us with six to eight leads per week, and that was good enough for my partner to turn down the job that would have required moving his family across the country and embark on the new 3.0 version of our business. It was April 2011, two weeks before I was to get married, and we were on the tailwind of two defunct businesses, spinning off now a third business venture and exposing our families to another span of twenty-plus-hour days to get the ball rolling. But this time, it felt different. This time there was peace—a calmness—that surrounded us. Maybe it was a calmness from knowing that if I failed, I'd find something new. Maybe it was a calmness because this chaos was my new norm. Or maybe it was a calmness that came from my newfound relationship with Jesus.

The Grind

In the past, it felt like it was us against the world, but this time it felt like it was someone else's plan, and we were along for the ride. It's hard to explain the difference, and at the time it wasn't apparent, but looking back and seeing how the pieces of the puzzle fell into place and how things came together, the only explanation for the calm was that for the first time in our entrepreneurial careers, we were following God's plan and not our own. I mentioned earlier how God comes to some in a burning bush as in Exodus 3:1–15:

> Now Moses was tending the flock of Jethro his father-in-law, the priest of Midian, and he led the flock to the far side of the wilderness and came to Horeb, the mountain of God. There the angel of the Lord appeared to him in flames of fire from within a bush. Moses saw that though the bush was on fire it did not burn up. So Moses thought, "I will go over and see this strange sight—why the bush does not burn up."
>
> When the Lord saw that he had gone over to look, God called to him from within the bush, "Moses! Moses!"
>
> And Moses said, "Here I am."
>
> "Do not come any closer," God said. "Take off your sandals, for the place where you are standing is holy ground." Then He said, "I am the God of your father, the God of Abraham, the God of Isaac and the God of Jacob." At this, Moses hid his face, because he was afraid to look at God.
>
> The Lord said, "I have indeed seen the misery of My people in Egypt. I have heard them crying out because of their slave drivers, and I am concerned about their suffering. So I have come down to rescue them from the hand of the Egyptians and to bring them up out of that

land into a good and spacious land, a land flowing with milk and honey—the home of the Canaanites, Hittites, Amorites, Perizzites, Hivites and Jebusites. And now the cry of the Israelites has reached Me, and I have seen the way the Egyptians are oppressing them. So now, go. I am sending you to Pharaoh to bring My people the Israelites out of Egypt."

But Moses said to God, "Who am I that I should go to Pharaoh and bring the Israelites out of Egypt?"

And God said, "I will be with you. And this will be the sign to you that it is I who have sent you: When you have brought the people out of Egypt, you will worship God on this mountain."

Moses said to God, "Suppose I go to the Israelites and say to them, 'The God of your fathers has sent me to you,' and they ask me, 'What is His name?' Then what shall I tell them?"

God said to Moses, "I AM WHO I AM. This is what you are to say to the Israelites: 'I AM has sent me to you.'"

God also said to Moses, "Say to the Israelites, 'The Lord, the God of your fathers—the God of Abraham, the God of Isaac and the God of Jacob—has sent me to you.'

"This is My name forever, the name you shall call Me, from generation to generation."

God cried out to Moses in such a way that you can't miss what He was trying to tell him to do. You cannot miss and you can't walk by or ignore a burning bush that is talking to you. But in life, how many opportunities do you miss, and how many times do you ignore the whisper? How many times do you pass up the seemingly small opportunities—the small nudges, the small things in life that *you* think are small, coincidences, fleeting thoughts, or even random ideas that could be God whispering to you to take control of your destiny? This is seen in one of my favorite Scriptures in the Bible, 1 Kings 19:9–18 (ESV):

> There he came to a cave and lodged in it. And behold, the word of the LORD came to him, and He said to him, "What are you doing here, Elijah?" He said, "I have been very jealous for the LORD, the God of hosts. For the people of Israel have forsaken Your covenant, thrown down Your altars, and killed Your prophets with the sword, and I, even I only, am left, and they seek my life, to take it away." And He said, "Go out and stand on the mount before the LORD." And behold, the LORD passed by, and a great and strong wind tore the mountains and broke in pieces the rocks before the LORD, but the LORD was not in the wind. And after the wind an earthquake, but the LORD was not in the earthquake. And after the earthquake a fire, but the LORD was not in the fire. And after the fire the sound of a low whisper. And when Elijah heard it, he wrapped his face in his cloak and went out and stood at the entrance of the cave. And behold, there came a voice to him and said, "What are you doing here, Elijah?" He said, "I have been very jealous for the LORD, the God of hosts. For the people of Israel have forsaken Your covenant, thrown down Your altars, and killed Your prophets with the sword, and I, even I only, am left, and they seek my life, to take it away." And the LORD said to him, "Go, return on your way to the wilderness of Damascus. And when you arrive, you shall anoint Hazael to be king over Syria. And Jehu the

son of Nimshi you shall anoint to be king over Israel, and Elisha the son of Shaphat of Abel-meholah you shall anoint to be prophet in your place. And the one who escapes from the sword of Hazael shall Jehu put to death, and the one who escapes from the sword of Jehu shall Elisha put to death. Yet I will leave seven thousand in Israel, all the knees that have not bowed to Baal, and every mouth that has not kissed him."

Unlike the burning bush, where God appears and calls out for Moses to come closer, these verses show the opposite—the Lord was not in the wind; the Lord was not in the earthquake; God was not in the fire. God shows in these Scriptures that He wants us to call on Him and to become so close to Him that even through the wind and the fire and the earthquakes, we will listen for His whisper. For the first time in my life, a whisper is what guided me.

It was the Monday before my wedding, April 11, 2011, and we officially had Total Home Roofing set up and were rolling out our new business. For comparison, we ended up with two clients during our first seven-day week in tax-prep operations, working off of "our plan." This gave us a whopping grand total of $462 in total revenue for a week's worth of work. In contrast, during the first five-day week of our roofing business (God's plan), we received eight new roofing leads and closed seven jobs, providing us with over $80,000 in revenue. This was proof enough for us. The whisper that had come to me while I slept was God. Just like Elijah, I could have been distracted and ignored the whisper. I had the earthquake of the business failure of our tax company, I had the sound of fire from the hectic stresses that come from planning a wedding, and I had the blowing of the wind distracting me as we managed to keep the other businesses afloat. All this could have drowned out the whisper—the calling and the direction of God's plan for our lives—if I hadn't listened.

What whispers have you heard? What earthquakes are rumbling in your life? Do you feel like you have a storm that is drowning out your calling? Is God calling you to step out from your current job? Do you have a passion in your heart to do more but a fear keeps you from going after it? Fear is not from God but the devil trying to hold you back from the glory God has in store for your life. All you have to do is listen to the whispers and act. If we look up the definition of the word *act*, *Oxford Languages* gives us two definitions that both fit with what God wants us to do:

1. act: take action, do something.
2. act: behave in the way specified.[5]

Second Timothy 1:7 (KJV) says, "For God hath not given us the spirit of fear; but of power, and of love, and of a sound mind." Just because you have had a setback—just because you have had a failure—doesn't mean that you give up. Failure is the only sure outcome of giving up. If we had quit after our mortgage business failed, we would have ignored the opportunity to start and build our tax company. If we had ignored the opportunity to start the tax franchise, it wouldn't have given us the knowledge and insight on building and running this business for God, which then blessed us with the opportunity to open a new company when He was ready. It's not our timing we have to remember—it's His timing. It's His plan. You just have to listen and act.

---

5. *Oxford Languages*, s.v. "act (*v.*)," accessed December 1, 2023.

CHAPTER 2

PLANNING

By failing to prepare, you are preparing to fail.
—Benjamin Franklin

If you are still reading this book, then it's safe to assume that you have heard the whisper—that voice inside you that's pulling at your emotions and is telling you there is more that the Word has to offer. As you dive into what God is calling you to do, I want to emphasize the importance of putting a plan in place to get you to your destination. When we started our tax franchise, we jumped in with two feet, and by dumb luck and by grinding it out, we made it but still ended up becoming a failed statistic. But looking back, what we realized at our corporate visit was the importance of *the plan*.

The plan is the invaluable asset that helps fast-track a business and allows you as the owner to focus all of your attention and efforts on the specific tasks needed to reach your goals. BusinessDIT released the following information in April 2023 on the importance of a business plan and how this plan is a critical tool for any entrepreneur wanting to launch a business.

A well-crafted business plan is a critical tool for any entrepreneur looking to successfully reach their goals. In fact, statistics show us that 71% of fast-growing businesses have written plans that they refer to often, while only 35% of smaller businesses take the time to create them.

Without a doubt, having a solid plan can be the difference between success and failure; other statistics back this up as well. Research reveals that businesses with plans tend to achieve over 2x more profits than those without.

Insightful Business Plan Success Statistics

1. Entrepreneurs with business plans are 260% more likely to launch.

2. A business plan increases the chances of growth by 30%.

3. Approximately 70% of businesses that survive for 5 years follow a strategic business plan.

4. 71% of fast-growing businesses have plans.

5. Compared to businesses without a written plan, those with one had a 7% higher likelihood of experiencing high growth.

6. One study found that only 35% of business owners who were surveyed had finished a business plan.

7. Simply put, business plan finishers were twice as likely to succeed.[1]

An effective business plan is your road map that lays out all your business goals in a clear, concise, organized, and

---

1. Yaqub M., "4 Business Plan Success Statistics You Need to Know," BusinessDIT, April 8, 2023, businessdit.com/business-plan-success-statistics/.

thought-out method that you and anyone involved in your business can follow. This road map is not something to keep private—this is something that everyone in your organization should be part of. Each person—each cog of the machine (your company)—works efficiently and effectively toward the clear goals established for your business.

Think of this as did Phil Jackson, coach of the 1990s Bulls. He effectively laid out a plan for the team and knew that to be successful, "Visions are never the sole property of one man or one woman. Before a vision can become reality, it must be owned by every single member of the group." Had we had the time to put a plan together before we jumped into our tax franchise with both feet, we would have been much more successful in year one. If we'd had a plan going into our first tax season, our efforts would have been better rewarded, and we would have had less chaos and stress trying to recreate the wheel.

This, our second business, started out with no plan, was chaotic, and ended up joining other failed businesses by closing its doors after just three years. In hindsight, when we established Total Home Roofing, we acted swiftly but methodically. We asked the questions that we needed to in order to establish a plan prior to jumping in with both feet so the effort that we were going to make could be directed to the goals we envisioned for this business. These directed goals fell in line with creating a business plan. The first plan that we established included a marketing plan, a financial plan, one-, two-, and three-year financial and sales projections, and a logistical wish-list plan that we created as a catchall for brain dumps and tweaks that we established along the way.

In the Bible, Proverbs 16:9 (NLT) shows us that "we can make our plans, but the LORD determines our steps." The base template for what we used, although not cookie-cutter in nature, enabled us to implement a quick, effective, and divisible plan to allow my partners and me to have a common objective, while working off of our own plans, to reach a mutually agreeable goal. These clear-cut goals were then easy to lay out and explain to our teams. Having clear, easy-to-understand, concise goals that allowed us as we grew our teams to gauge performance and be part of the successes and failures made for a symbiotic relationship that inspired and drove everyone toward this mutually recognized goal.

Sounds simple enough, doesn't it? No need to read any more if you can take this one tidbit and implement it in your business. Then you will increase your probability of success drastically. What we found during our failures (yes, multiple) is that businesses need very specific and key goals. Once these goals are established, the team needs to be able to track their performance to see that they are contributing and are part of the team that is working toward and accomplishing these goals. If you make the goals too hard to understand, if you make them unclear, or if you don't have the direction or communication skills to clearly outline your goals so that your team knows what they are working toward and sees the progress, then you and your team will flail. Think of these goals as the elevator discussion of what you want to see your business do. These are the ten commandments for the business. Everyone signs off on these commandments as absolutes.

When I say *everyone*, this doesn't mean that you have to have fifty people in your organization. This can be you and your cat. Just make sure that your cat's going to be okay with what you put down as your goal. If your goal means you are gone for a month and your cat won't eat, then your goal for your business won't line up with your life, and you will not be able to effectively reach this goal because outside constraints will keep you from doing what you committed yourself to do.

Once you have established these absolutes, then each person grabs the reins on his or her list of tasks and has at it. Once you know what you're doing, it's easy to go all in, full send, do not look back, head down, and grind it out. What this allows is full control and focus over a smaller set of activities that each person in the organization can focus on at the micro level. You can focus your attention 100 percent on achieving these goals, and you can develop KPIs (key performance indicators) to make sure your plan is on track. This also allows your business to get out of its own way. You eliminate the minutia that slows your business down. You eliminate the negative input from parties that aren't the best at making the individual decisions at hand. These negative inputs stifle the entrepreneurial excitement and ability to tweak as needed along the way to make sure that your business is operating at maximum efficiency.

In our case, we created three individual business segments that operated 100 percent independently from each other with a common goal, guided by the commandments set in place to reach the final destination. I'll break this down in better detail. I am a finance guy. I have an MBA in advanced finance. I see in numbers; I talk in numbers; I understand numbers. So, intuitively, I took over the business and finance side of the company.

My other partners' pieces of the pie included partner one: sales and marketing. He is the best person that I know at sales and marketing. His decisions, what he sees, and how he looks at things are far superior to my financial mind trying to put together sales and marketing. So why should I be involved in those decisions? It stifles his ability to do his best. It's like telling Michael Jordan to dribble a certain way—a way different from what he's already doing. Why do it? Give him the ball and get out of his way.

Finishing out our three-piece pie, my third partner has a mind for production. He is the Yoda of production—managing crews, getting jobs completed, quality control—all of it. Why in the world would finance Rob or marketing man get in the way of Yoda running production? There is no reason to.

"If you meet Buddha in the paint, pass him the ball" is another Phil Jackson quote. If you don't get the basketball analogies, what he's saying is if you see someone that can do it or is more talented than you, then pass that player the ball. Understand that you are not the best at everything. The reality is that you and I, and my partners, are probably not the best at anything—much less everything. So, if you come across anyone that is better than you at something, then pass them the ball. Give them the task, let them run with it, and get out of their way. You then can focus on what you do "good, better, or best" and let them pass you the ball on those tasks.

This simple concept allowed us to all work at 100 percent toward the common goal that we had in place. I developed budgets for the departments based on our mutual goals for the growth of the company for the first, second, third, and fifth years. We ran our departments based off these budgets.

We had the budget, we knew our pricing, and marketing knew what they had to sell jobs and what they could spend to make the phones ring. Production knew what they could spend on production, warranty, and greasing the squeaky wheels that arise in any business, and I could manage cash flow and most importantly make sure that we put money in our employees' and owners' pockets. It was a beautiful thing. Edwin Louis Cole once said, "There are dreamers and there are planners; the planners make their dreams come true." We were turning our dreams into reality, and God was determining each and every step along the way.

CHAPTER 3

ACTION VS. MOVEMENT

I have found so many instances in which success or failure comes down to slight details—just like in the words *action* and *movement*. When we look at the words on the surface, they appear to be very similar. *Action* is moving. *Movement* is also moving, but when we take a deeper look at the true meaning of each word—if you break down the details—it can mean the difference between whether you succeed or fail.

Why are the details so important? Well, the numbers don't lie. In research by LendingTree, it was found that 20.8 percent of private-sector businesses fail within the first year. After five years, this percentage jumps to 48.4 percent, and after ten years, over 65 percent of businesses in the U.S. have failed. Reading these statistics, entrepreneurs should be aware that the odds are stacked against them in becoming successful in business. This is why the details—the minutia, for lack of a better word—can make the difference between whether your business thrives or dies.[1]

---

1. Devon Delfino, "The Percentage of Businesses that Fail—and How to Boost Your Chances of Success," LendingTree, May 8, 2023, lendingtree.com/business/small/failure-rate/.

So, let's get into the details. What does *movement* truly mean? According to *Oxford Languages, movement* is "the general activity or bustle of people or things in a particular place."[2] In business terms, this means that movement is effort without progress. Movement is any effort given on any activity, or any hour spent, that has no direction and does not give direct progress toward the goal at hand. It is any effort or time given to activities that are not specifically moving you or your business forward on the plan that was established.

Action, on the other hand, is effort with a meaningful objective. *Oxford Languages* defines *action* as "the fact or process of doing something, typically to achieve an aim,"[3] or a goal. So, why devote an entire chapter to breaking down the seemingly minute details and differences between these two words? you might be asking. The reason is that although it appears these words are similar, this is where business owners get caught up in thinking they are "building their business" when they are really just wasting their and their teams' time. This is where the rubber meets the road. This is where the scorecard of a business is exposed for the world to see. Those that are taking action will be shown through their entrepreneurial successes. Those that are just moving without progress will be excited to share their newly designed business cards to all their friends and family while their businesses flail and don't produce or provide for society.

The question you have to ask yourself is, Where do you want to be? Cameron Haynes, extreme Ultra athlete, bow hunter, adventurer, etc., coined the phrase, "Do hard sh*t."

---

2. *Oxford Languages*, s.v. "movement (*n.*)," accessed December 4, 2023.
3. Ibid., s.v. "action (*n.*)," accessed December 4, 2023.

Action vs. Movement

It's simple. To be successful, you have to *do*. You have to be willing to do the hard stuff that the other people don't want to do. If you want to sit in your office and design your business card, that's great, but don't trick yourself into thinking that you are taking action in your business and that you had a productive day. You may have spent eight hours in your office, but the effort you expended—the movement that was made—did not move the needle of success on your business.

If your business plan is littered with movement items like "create business card," you will not be successful. Your business will fail. You will not taste the victory of being a business that survives the one-, two-, three-, five-, or ten-year mark. Don't waste your time. You have to do the hard sh*t. Do the stuff that your competitors are not willing to do. This doesn't mean stand on your head or walk across burning coals. This means embrace the things that aren't inherently fun. You have to grind it out. You have to wake up every morning with a single goal in mind, and that goal is to move the needle of your business forward. In any way, shape, or form, you are going to move it forward no matter how hard it is.

This means your mindset changes from a time clock to a scorecard. Anyone can punch a time clock, wasting away another eight-hour day at the office or working in their business. Yes, you can also convince yourself, your wife or husband, and your friends that you are working on your business. But if you didn't produce—if you didn't move your business forward—then all you did was make movement from your bed to your office and back again. Don't fake yourself out.

Primitive man had a much easier scorecard to display. He went hunting, he caught food, he ate. Business owners today need to bring back the primal instincts of hunting and gathering of their ancestors. When you lay your head down at night, what have you brought back to camp? Are you eating the sweet taste of meat? Did you find some berries? Or are you sitting around camp cleaning toilets, waiting for someone else to bring dinner back to you? Stop being someone who is waiting for berries to show up—you have to go out and get them.

Here is the reality—it isn't going to just happen. Jerry Rice once said, "Today I will do what others won't, so tomorrow I can do what others can't." This is where your plan takes your movements and turns them into actions. Each step of your plan has been established. Now, all you have to do is make sure that your movements reflect the goals of your plan. With each movement made—each task taken on—each hour of your day must be filled with movements that are focused on the plan as laid out. These strategic movements turn into your action steps that execute your plan. Anything that doesn't move your plan forward ends up getting knocked off your to-do list. It's not a part of the action plan. It's a movement, a filler, a time suck. It will not make your business successful, and it will not move you forward. This is where your plan and your actions come together. Each action that you make will have quantifiable impact on your business plan. I.e., each action step accomplished will move your business forward.

For example, your company has a sales goal of $50,000. An action plan to reach this goal will look something like this:

- It costs me X dollars or X time spent to generate a lead.

- I need X number of leads to generate an appointment (or X number of clicks).
- I need X number of appointments to generate a sale.
- I need X number of sales at average price to reach my sales goal.

Now you have a quantifiable system that will track your activity. This then turns into a simple math problem from which you can work backwards. Any business at any stage should be able to implement this system and this type of tracking system in their KPIs to not only monitor action vs. movement of the organization but to also forecast and to adjust projections of the business for short- and long-term goals. If you are a one-person business, this action plan is simple. If you're starting out, you can get industry averages for your business for sales prices of products and services and the average closing percentage for qualified leads. A quick google search of your industry will give you the two numbers that you need, and you can base your ability (are you a sales genius or not so good at sales?) to tweak the estimated percentage of success for your closing percentage. For example:

- Average sale price: $5,000
- Closing percentage: 25%

This means if you have a goal of $50,000 per month in sales, you will need to sell ten jobs.

- $50,000 per month sales goal = $5,000 average job cost x 10

If you need to sell ten jobs and you have a 25 percent closing percentage (or an industry average of 25 percent if you are putting together a plan just starting out):

- 10 jobs at 25% closing percentage = 40 leads needed

Now that you know how many leads are needed to meet your goal, you have to figure out the cost for these leads in advertising, or the time needed to generate these leads. For example, if you can purchase leads through online advertising, these companies will give you the estimate conversion rate of clicks-to-website to leads. If they quote you two dollars per click and you need one hundred clicks to convert to a lead, we use simple math again:

- $2 per click x 100 clicks needed per lead = $200 per lead

To reach your goal, you need forty leads, as we see from the formula above.

- 40 leads needed x $200 cost per lead = $8,000 advertising budget per month

Now we can develop KPIs:

- $8,000 a month in advertising to generate $50,000 in revenue
- $8,000 / $50,000 = 16 percent of gross revenue will be spent on advertising

Is this number viable in your business? I don't know. I don't know what business you have. If you're building websites and you have no material costs, then probably yes. If you are doing construction and materials cost 50 percent of your sale, then maybe not. For the example above, it doesn't matter. The example shows you how to lay out the action plan for your business so that you know that the movements that you are making are becoming actions toward the plan you have in place.

In the example above, you realize that you need forty leads per month to reach your goal. So, each day, you need to monitor the progress of reaching this goal. Is your advertising working? Can you do something to improve it? The leads come in, and then you need to execute on these leads to ensure that you are reaching your anticipated closing percentage. If not, then you need to work on a new action plan. Sales training, sales techniques, closing strategies—all these things become new tasks to add to your daily to-do list until you meet your intended KPI goals.

Once your goals are met for a certain action item, then you can focus your attention on the next action item. The goal is that your daily activities morph into planned activities that are moving your business in the direction of your goals. All the activities tie together. All the time spent is productive, all the hours invested are used to benefit and build off the plan that's in place. You have now compartmentalized your schedule—your daily planner—with activities that are productive. No longer will you wake up and think, What will I do today? Your plan has already shown you what needs to be done. You now have the information at hand to generate your own internal scorecard. No longer will you flail through the day. Now you can easily track your success.

> Public Service Announcement: You may realize that you are not cut out for this. I say this with love. It's not to be mean. It's fine if you can't look in the mirror and promise yourself that you will grind it out, but don't lie to yourself, your family, and your friends. If you can't wake up every morning and do the hard stuff, then stop reading and go find something else to do with your life.

Save yourself and your loved ones the stress and heartache of you sitting in your office pretending that you are building a business or moving the needle forward when you are just wasting your time and not bettering the life of your family.

Are you bringing home the meat and berries, or are you starving tonight? Set up a simple Excel formula to track your day, week, month, and year performance. If you want to start a business and don't know what Excel is, stop reading this book now and as a step one, familiarize yourself with Excel. (If you don't have Microsoft Excel, then use Google Sheets. If you don't have a computer, then go get a computer. If you don't know how to use it, ask any ten-year-old kid to show you the basics so you can start to figure it out, or hire someone to do it for you.) Your tracker can be as simple as the one below and can easily be tweaked to add or subtract additional items that are worthwhile to track on a daily, weekly, and monthly basis.

Day	Clicks	Leads	Sales	Revenue
1	77	0	0	0
2	91	0	0	0
3	41	0	0	0
4	62	1	1	$5,000
5	12	1	0	0
(to be continued...)				
Total	283	2	1	$5,000
Goal	4,000	40	10	$50,000
% to Goal	7%	7.5%	10%	10%

Tracking your daily action plan gives you a sense of accomplishment and small wins. It allows activity to breed activity. It allows you to see the minor changes on a day-to-day basis that are creating momentum toward the larger goal. These small wins—these small movements forward in your action plan—help generate motivation and show success. Without recording what you are doing, what is working, and what isn't working, you have no scorecard to know if your plan is working, if it's successful, or if you set your goals too low and need to adjust them higher. You can't become a billion-dollar company without first becoming a million-dollar company. Tracking what works and what does not work will allow you to tweak your goals and keep yourself on track each and every day to ensure you and your team are spending time on the action steps necessary to propel your business forward.

CHAPTER 4

LEADERSHIP

Leadership is not about forcing your will on others.
It's about mastering the art of letting go.
—Phil Jackson

It's good to be the boss! This is what I thought when I started Island Heritage Contractors. I was twenty-four years old and ready to take on the world. I had my vision and my plan in place. I was in control of my destiny, and I was going to revolutionize the real estate and construction industries. My partner at the time was managing the day-to-day field operations, and I was running the business and finance portions of the business. We had our systems down pat and were successfully growing our company. We brought on an in-home sales associate, a permitting and scheduling coordinator, and full-time field employees to help control the construction projects and offer a smooth turnkey approach to remodeling. Things were firing on all cylinders, and we experienced a fair amount of success in the first year of this business.

In year two, we realized we had achieved a double-edged sword. We were experiencing business growth, but with each stage of growth, my partner and I both took on more and more responsibility to ensure we kept the promises and the quality that our reputation was built on. I was twenty-five years old. I was running a successful construction company, I was building and running a mortgage-origination business, and I was developing and building a real estate company. With each expansion, with each growth, with each new employee that was hired, I assumed another feather in my hat and another responsibility to add to my to-do list each day. I had my partner, who shared in the workload and absorbed as much of the added responsibility as he possibly could. But the realization slowly set in that the processes and procedures that we'd built and set in motion were either going to kill us or we were going to slow the growth of the business. We could only do so much, and even less could we actually do well.

This stress caused turmoil in our company. By 2007, the stress had gotten so bad that my partner approached me to buy him out of the business. Looking back, it should have been a red flag for me, but my mentality was and had always been to go full send on anything and everything I did. I saw this instead as a new challenge that I needed to overcome. I happily bought him out and added yet another set of tasks to my list. When I turned twenty-seven, I was working sixteen-hour days, six days a week, nonstop. My work-life balance was zero. I was averaging one hundred-plus calls a day, and I was emailing and scheduling jobs—along with submitting real estate offers and mortgage applications between ten and eleven p.m. so that they would be in the listing agents' and lenders' inboxes first thing in the morning.

Leadership

I have battled with chronic sinus issues ever since I was a little kid. I was a walking ENT science experiment, from tonsils, to adenoids, to tubes in my ears, etc.—you name it, I had it. As a teenager and adult, I dealt with chronic sinus infections. When I say chronic, I mean *double Z-Pak, get done with one sinus infection, wait thirty days, rinse, and repeat*-type of sinus infections. Then the realization hit me. It was on a day in the summer of 2007 that I finally realized I couldn't do what I was doing anymore. I couldn't get out of bed. I couldn't answer the phone. I couldn't even open my eyes. This was the reality of the situation at hand. Everything that I had built was dependent on me to keep it moving. I had built the highest-demanding job I ever could have created when I thought that I was building companies. I was wrong.

I only knew one thing. I knew how to be the center of the activity and how to create jobs and hire employees that were dependent on me. I knew that if I took responsibility for a project, a timeline, and a goal, that it would be done. I had my team in place, and they worked hard, but they had no clear vision, no clear goals, and no clear manual for success. I had taught them to come to me with any questions, comments, or concerns, and I would help. Now, as I lay here hopeless in bed and things were crumbling around me, I realized the errors and the mistakes I had made.

It took me three days to recover and to get back on my feet. Part of it was sinus infection, and the other part was pure exhaustion from ninety- to one hundred-hour weeks for the last two years. I'd mentally and physically had enough, and I couldn't do it anymore. It's funny how life has a way to letting you make your own mistakes. Then, when you're done getting your teeth kicked in, your brain starts to work and gives you a new clarity.

That morning when I went into the office, I took aside my first employee, who had been with me from day one. I told him that from that day, "I need you to be my project manager. I can't do it anymore, and I know you can. If you have any issues, you make the decision. Good or bad—make the decision, and I'll back you. You do what you think is right and in the best interest of the customer. At the end of each day, we'll talk and run through the schedule, and anything that you couldn't make go away, we'll come up with a plan for it."

Like that, one thing was off my list. When my office manager came in, I explained to her the same thing. She was a hybrid employee, helping expedite admin duties across all three companies. I gave her a similar spiel. The new goal in the office was that if a customer called us, someone didn't do their job. Our goal now was to update all customers and keep them updated with enough information that they never needed to call us. Whether that was a call, email, text, etc., if an existing customer contacted my cell phone or the office, then we hadn't done our job.

Overnight, my call load went from one hundred-plus calls a day to twenty. The twenty calls I got were important calls—calls that really needed my attention—and I now had the time and the freedom to devote to these calls vs. rushing off the phone to answer the next incoming call.

So, what's the importance of my pity-party story of how I caused my own stress in my own life, and how does this help you? Through the ninety-hour weeks and the turmoil in my health and sanity, I finally realized that everything hung on just letting go. By letting go of the reins, I created a working environment that allowed the great employees that I had to harness their full potential. Empowering them to make their own decisions created an environment where they felt they had value and were building and contributing to something bigger than themselves. By allowing them the freedom to pave their own paths, I opened up the door for them to create a work environment that they enjoyed being in. I was able to bring sanity and balance back into my life, and my employees went from stressed-out dependent employees to empowered, vested, highly valued members of the organization. When I say this, I mean this from the bottom of my heart.

The turning point in my business life was the realization that people want to be part of something bigger than themselves—to wake up to purpose, to feel like what they are doing is contributing to the greater good, that they are building something. This is where true leadership comes in—guiding someone to their best ability and allowing them to create and to bring value to the table even though their ideas may not be the same as your ideas as the owner or not the way that you would do things. The team becomes the power source of the business, and you as the leader just guide it in the direction that you need it to go.

You don't need to micromanage. If you feel the need to micromanage, then either you are doing something wrong as the leader, or you chose the wrong employee to fill the position. Either way, look in the mirror and realize it's your fault. Not their fault. It's never their fault.

This method of managing—this leadership ability—has allowed me to build and retain employees in some of the highest-turnover industries in the U.S. We have employees of our construction company that have been here for over a decade and still to this day say it's the best job and the best place to work they could ever ask for. We have acted as an incubator for our employees to go off on their own to start their own companies. We support them and mentor them through the steps to prevent the turmoil that I experienced and to help them navigate a path less bumpy than the one I made. To date, we have incubated nine spin-off companies from past employees who were looking for an opportunity to better their lives and the lives of their families.

When I share these success stories with my coaching clients, I'll get a sideways look, which says something along the lines of, "I don't want the extra competition in my business. I'm not helping someone compete against me," or, "Why would I help someone start a business that I don't have ownership in?" I've learned not to respond with anything more than to read Deuteronomy 28:11–12 (NLT):

> The LORD will give you prosperity in the land He swore to your ancestors to give you, blessing you with many children, numerous livestock, and abundant crops. The LORD will send rain at the proper time from His rich treasury in the heavens and will bless all the work you do.

In life, you can have an abundance mindset or a scarcity mindset. The choice is yours. If you feel like you won't have enough business and one more competitor will undermine your business, you're probably right. If you have an abundance mindset, then you will realize that there is more work out there than you and the person that you are helping will be able to handle. The mental choice is yours. What kind of working environment do you envision? What type of working environment would you want to work in? If you were an employee working for someone else, how would you like to be treated? When you answer these questions and you put your thoughts in place and the pieces of your plan together, all I ask is that you don't make the same mistakes I did.

I was fortunate to realize this at a young age—before I had a family and before I was married. I was able to transition my thinking and my actions to allow me to build and manage and grow successful businesses and enrich the lives of the employees that worked in them. As business owners, we have the duty and the responsibility to create value for the world, to create value for our employees, and to create value for ourselves. If we focus on any one of these three while ignoring the others, the business will fall apart. These parts are woven together and equally important in their impact on our ability to start, build, grow, and flourish in business.

Don't lose sight of this as things grow and change, and never lose sight of the fact that the employees are more important to the business than you. First Peter 5:5 (NLT) tells us:

> In the same way, you who are younger must accept the authority of the elders. And all of you, dress yourselves in humility as you relate to one another, for "God opposes the proud but gives grace to the humble."

CHAPTER 5

THE GREAT I AM

I went back and forth on the name of this chapter up until the final edit of this book. The other chapter title was going to be "The Great Divide." This title seemed to bring out a passionately strong opinion from the people I talked with while writing this book—so much so that I almost cut out the whole chapter. Instead, I kept it short and sweet.

When I say the words "The great I AM," what comes to your mind? Fifty percent of the time, the new business owner or entrepreneur sitting across from me will smile, lift their hand, stick out their thumb, point it at their chest, and say, "Me!" To this, I smirk, nod my head, and continue to ask a couple of more questions. It's true that many of the business owners that we mentioned in chapter 1 that have become household names portray themselves as being the great I AM. They are the founders of worldwide companies, they employ thousands of employees, and they create products that span the globe. But when it all comes down to it, is their success truly because of them?

The Bible says in Proverbs 16:9 (NLT): "We can make our plans, but the LORD determines our steps." If the Lord determines your steps, then by deductive reasoning, it's safe to assume that He is part of your business. If He plans your steps, then how can you get anywhere without Him? You may have a great idea. You may have a great thought—a vision even—or a plan. But it is God that determines your steps. How can He determine your steps if He isn't part of your life? If He is part of your life planning at each and every step, then how could He not be part of your business? So, if God controls each step of your life and He is responsible for each step of your business, then how can you think that you are the great I Am? For, He is the great I Am.

God

Employees

You

Once we have established the hierarchy of our business organization, the pieces of the puzzle fall into place. As entrepreneurs, we can't do it alone. We need to take on the servant mindset and realize that we are following God's plan. It is God who is preparing the path for us, and He has blessed us with being the stewards (or the servants) that are implementing His plan. This mindset is one in which our businesses need God first, employees second, and us third.

From my experience building businesses now for twenty years, I have found that I have greater success under God's plan than under my plan. I tried taking control of my company and running a business with myself as the center of all things, and I almost ended up in the hospital. It was only when I revised my organizational hierarchy, putting God and my employees first, that I truly realized peace in my businesses. Matthew 11:28–30 (NLT) tells us:

> Then Jesus said, "Come to Me, all of you who are weary and carry heavy burdens, and I will give you rest. Take My yoke upon you. Let Me teach you, because I am humble and gentle at heart, and you will find rest for your souls. For My yoke is easy to bear, and the burden I give you is light."

CHAPTER 6

B.B.B. (BUILDING BUSINESS BIBLICALLY)

In 2005, I started my first professional business. (I say this was my first business because my lawn-service business back in 1993–96 didn't have any employees.) The incredible feeling of starting a company is that you can make it anything that you want it to be. The goals, the values, the employees, the logo, the products—all of these things are up to you and your vision. You get to create all the rules. You can follow in the footsteps of others and build your company to look like other companies that influence you, or you can flip an industry upside down by approaching your company differently. You take the culmination of all the character traits that have been instilled in you, what drives you personally to move forward, and what you feel the world needs most to develop your new mission statement and business plan.

For myself, this meant looking back at the teachings from my mom when I was a preteen—the values of hard work, dedication, and the striving for perfection in all that you do, along with the pursuit of efficiency to eliminate waste. I also built off the teachings of my first boss. He taught me that a business is a tool. Your product responds to a need that you see and is the opportunity that comes from filling that need. The business can morph, and the products can change over time as you build your business, but the fundamentals and core values that your business is built on are the most important aspect in positioning your company for success.

Throughout the Scriptures, we read in many different places of the Biblical principles that God established for us in regard to living our lives financially and how to handle our business dealings. Being good stewards of our finances, saving, and growing our businesses ethically, morally, and according to the Word of the Lord show us how to serve God and others along our path.

These Biblical principles are the building blocks of the mission statements of some of the most respected businesses today. These owners see the value and the power of aligning themselves, their businesses, and their employees with godly principles through their mission statements and what standing in faith with God will do. The results are some of the most incredible businesses that the world has ever seen—companies that employees love to work for, customers are drawn to, and which have in some cases changed history by keeping their faith in God, putting Him first, standing strong, and believing that all things are possible through Him.

- Proverbs 13:11: "Dishonest money dwindles away, but whoever gathers money little by little makes it grow."
- Proverbs 28:20 (NASB): "A faithful man will abound with blessings, but he who makes haste to be rich will not go unpunished."

- Psalm 112:5 (ESV): "It is well with the man who deals generously and lends; who conducts his affairs with justice."
- Luke 16:10 (NASB): "He who is faithful in a very little thing is faithful also in much; and he who is unrighteous in a very little thing is unrighteous also in much."

In all these Scriptures, God shows us the character traits that are needed to be successful in life and in business: honesty, not being hasty, being generous to others, being faithful and righteous, treating others the way we want to be treated, and standing faithful in our beliefs. These traits in themselves, when wisely applied to business interactions of the world, set companies apart from the rest.

During the span of the last fifteen years, I have built several businesses, conducted countless real estate transactions, hired hundreds of employees, and consulted hundreds on managing their personal and business finances. My fundamental findings about those that are successful and those that struggle can be traced back to the principles of the Bible. When I discuss planning and goal setting or setting up a business plan with a business owner, I use a formula that explains exactly what this means. It breaks down the internal values of the entrepreneur to their core to get the true *why* of their mission statement and their plan. You will see that the formula below breaks down such that success is the sum of your faith plus your values multiplied by your work output.

While putting together a business plan, I developed a twenty-question questionnaire that will give a score on each of the inputs for faith and values on a scale of one to five. The work input is based on your ability to actually commit to your business's success. This is the input that you, the owner-operator of this business, control. This is where you can decide to work twenty hours a week or one hundred hours a week to help determine your outcome. The other inputs are based on your vision and your values for the business—how closely do they align with those in the Bible and how closely do you align yourself with godly principles to give glory to God through your work?

- Success = (Faith + Values) x (Work Output)

This formula breaks down like this: Your success is the total of all things working together in your business. Your faithfulness in the Lord and putting Him first are critical points in your business. Some people ask, "Is this required? I'm a good person, and I have good values. I just don't know where I stand with God." Well, no, it isn't required, but without putting the Lord first and partnering with Him, you add an exponential amount of work to your plate. In essence, you have the option of your way or Yahweh, as I like to say.

Here is an example of how the formula works without faith: We will call this Tim's business. Tim answers the questionnaire, and the results give him scores of:

- Faith = 1
- Values = 5

Tim is young and hungry and wants to be successful in life. He has decided on and committed to a plan of doing whatever it takes to be successful and puts forth a plan committing that he will work six days a week, eight hours per day. So, Tim has a forty-eight-hour time commitment with which to develop his business. Now that we have all his inputs, we simply put them into the formula:

- Success = (1 [Faith] + 5 [Values]) x (48 [Hours])

Tim's success score for his business plan is 288.

Let's now take a look at Joe's business. Joe is a faithful man of God, and when he comes to me to discuss his plan, we go through the same questions that we did with Tim, but Joe's scores and his answers are very different from Tim's. Joe ends up with scores of:

- Faith = 4
- Values = 4
- Work = 40
- Success = (4 [Faith] + 4 [Values]) x (40 [Hours])

Joe's success score for his business plan is 320.

From the outside looking in, Tim seems to have a higher commitment to his business than Joe. Tim is willing to commit to working one additional day per week to make his company successful, and he displays the highest value score that he could get—meaning that his intentions are good for his employees and customers. What he lacks, though, is the compounding effect of putting the Lord first. By partnering with God in his business and allowing Him to act as his partner, Tim has to work that much harder to be successful. How much harder? you ask. Great question. To figure that out, we work backwards off this formula. For Tim to reach Joe's success score of 320:

- 320 = (1 [Faith] + 5 [Values]) x (X)

To find X, we simply take 320 and divide the sum of (Faith + Values), which is 6.

- 320/6 = X (53.33 Hours)

By not partnering with God, Tim will have to drastically increase his work commitment of forty-eight hours per week if he wants to meet the success-rate score of 320 in Joe's plan (Joe is working only forty hours per week). Tim now has to work 53.33 hours per week to reach this same level for probability of success. Tim's effort of 13.33 hours more than Joe results in him needing to do 33 percent more work to reach the same goal. By trying to do things on his own in his way, without God's help and partnership, Tim has to work twenty minutes more every hour to keep pace.

Or, looking at this inversely, Joe's forty-hour-per-week commitment will result in 53.33 hours of production in his business by partnering with God. Now, about this time I usually get the argument, "Rob, this can't be a scientific formula. There is no way that this can be broken down and proved hour per hour to be accurate." To all the naysayers, I challenge you to try it your way. According to Investopedia.com, 20 percent of businesses fail in the first year, 50 percent within five years, and 65 percent by the tenth year.[1]

These statistics prove that the ways of the world make it incredibly hard for business owners to become successful, and even if they experience success in the beginning, they may not last the course of time. I for one would rather have a partner on my side that knows the course. In Jeremiah 29:11, the Lord tells us the plan He has for our lives if we just have faith in Him: "'For I know the plans I have for you,' declares the LORD, 'plans to prosper you and not to harm you, plans to give you hope and a future.'"

---

1. Sean Bryant, "How Many Startups Fail and Why?," Investopedia, November 26, 2022, accessed December 18, 2023, investopedia.com/articles/personal-finance/040915/how-many-startups-fail-and-why.asp.

To give an illustration, I love to use the metaphor of racing. Usain Bolt is the fastest person on the planet. At top speed, it's calculated that he runs at a speed of 23.35 mph. This is an incredible feat in comparison to the average person, whose estimated top running speed (based on 100m) is 15 mph.

Putting this in perspective with our example above, we see that Joe's plan is that of a normal, average person. A forty-hour-workweek commitment is equal to the average person's running ability of 15 mph. This is something that is possible for almost everyone. Being the average, some will be slightly higher, and some will be slightly lower. But in general, everyone should be able to achieve this rate of physical performance in their life.

On the other hand, Tim needs to perform at a much higher rate. His output needs to be 33 percent higher than the average (15 mph + 33% = 19.95 mph). This output and the toll on his body lead to a multitude of issues. They take time away from work-life balance, and they cause stress due to working 33 percent harder than competitors. There is the added strain of burnout, and the most disheartening issue may be when you break down the pay.

When interviewing business owners, most of them have worked for other employers at some point in life in an hourly position. I'm sure most of you are familiar with this type of employment, in which for each hour worked you receive X dollars.

- Paycheck = Hours Worked x Hourly Pay

I.e., I trade one hour of work for x number of predetermined dollars or other currency.

With our success formula for forecasting, we take the industry norm, or average (as in the running example), to determine a business owner's projected income per year, and the success score is the probability of them reaching that goal with their business in the future. In the examples of Tim's and Joe's businesses, let's say for example that they are both in the same business of selling widgets. In this widget business, we find that the average business in this industry has revenue of $1,000,000 per year and that the average net margin is 10 percent (in this example we will assume that net profit results in owner's pay).

- $1,000,000 Revenue Yearly
- $100,000 10% net (Owner's Pay)

To factor output, we take hours worked per week, multiply that by fifty-two weeks per year, and divide that number by owner's pay to find out how profitable their output is.

Tim's Output

- 53.33 hours per week x 52 = 2,773 hours (rounded)
- $100,000 owner's pay / 2,773 hours worked = $36.06 per hour

Joe's Output

- 40 hours per week x 52 = 2,080 hours
- $100,000 owner pay / 2,080 hours worked = $48.08 per hour

In both examples, our owners are blessed to have a six-figure income at the end of the year, but in the example, Tim has to work so much harder—693 additional hours, to be exact—to get to the same outcome. At this point in our meeting, I'm typically met with, "Rob, I hear what you are saying, but I am the best salesman, best construction guy, best finance guy, best realtor. People love me. It's not going to be that way for me in my business." At this point I smile. You might be the best in your field, but you are not greater than God. It's much better to rely on His strengths than your own strengths. Imagine if you used your gifts coupled with His gifts—where do you think your business would be? We discussed it before—I will bet on Yahweh over your way every single time.

My favorite example of this in business is Chick-fil-A. From the outside looking in, this is a fast-food restaurant that just makes a chicken sandwich. Now, when talking with people about the success of this restaurant, they explain it by saying that the quality is better, or the restaurant is cleaner, or the staff is happier, which is of course part of the culture that they strive for and have built. But to truly understand why they are in this position, we have to look back at what their mission statement reads and what they are built on:

> Chick-fil-A founder S. Truett Cathy is a devout Christian who has taught Sunday School for over 51 years and whose religious beliefs permeate the company to this day. The company's official statement of corporate purpose says that the business exists "to glorify God by being a faithful steward of all that is entrusted to us and to have a positive influence on all who come in contact with Chick-fil-A." The chain invests heavily in community services (especially for children and teenagers) and scholarships. Cathy's beliefs are also responsible for one of the chain's distinctive features: All Chick-fil-A

locations (company-owned and franchised, whether in a mall or freestanding) are closed on Sundays.[2]

Chick-fil-A's mission is "to glorify God" first and foremost. I like to compare it to the McDonald's mission statement. Now, McDonald's is the largest fast-food restaurant and arguably one of the biggest brands ever created, with locations across the globe. The McDonald's mission statement is:

> Our mission is to make delicious feel-good moments easy for everyone....[3]
>
> This is how we uniquely feed and foster communities. We serve delicious food people feel good about eating, with convenient locations and hours and affordable prices, and by working hard to offer the speed, choice and personalization our customers expect. At our best, we don't just serve food, we serve moments of feel-good, all with the lighthearted, unpretentious, welcoming, dependable personality consumers know and love.[4]

Here we see two companies, two global brands, and two completely different models. Chick-fil-A has chosen "to glorify God." McDonald's has chosen to "serve moments of feel-good." Both companies are extremely successful global brands, but only one has the purpose "to glorify God."

"Humility is the fear of the LORD; its wages are riches and honor and life" (Proverbs 22:4). For glorifying the Lord, the Bible promises riches and honor and life, so let's compare our

---

2. "Religious Connections," Chick-fil-A Wiki, accessed December 6, 2023, chickfila.fandom.com/wiki/Religious_Connections.

3. "Who We Are," McDonald's, accessed December 6, 2023, corporate.mcdonalds.com/corpmcd/our-company/who-we-are.html.

4. "Our Mission and Values," McDonald's, accessed December 6, 2023, corporate.mcdonalds.com/corpmcd/our-company/who-we-are/our-values.html.

two favorite restaurants just like we broke down Tim's and Joe's companies and efforts above.'

McDonald's
- Average Annual Store Revenue: $2,700,00
- Open 365 days a year
- Average Daily Revenue: $7,397.26

Chick-fil-A
- Average Annual Store Revenue: $4,200,000
- Open 312 days a year (closed Sundays and Christmas)
- Average Daily Revenue: $13,461.54

Comparison: McDonald's is open fifty-three more days per year, operating their business 15 percent more than Chick-fil-A. Chick-fil-A per-store revenue is 1.56 times higher on average (56 percent) than that of McDonald's. Chick-fil-A daily revenue is 1.82 times higher than McDonald's (82 percent).

The results are astonishing. How can a business work 15 percent less but generate 1.5 times the sales in a given year? Just like we saw in the success calculator above in the stories of Joe and Tim, Chick-fil-A was founded on the principle of putting God first and operates under the blessing of and partnership with the Lord. By positioning yourself and aligning your hard work and values with the Lord, the Lord provides. In Exodus, the Lord talks about obeying the Sabbath:

> Bear in mind that the LORD has given you the Sabbath; that is why on the sixth day He gives you bread for two days. Everyone is to stay where they are on the seventh day; no one is to go out. (Exodus 16:29)

So, if you honor the Lord's commands regarding the Sabbath, the Lord gives you two days' worth of provision. It's interesting to note that as in Exodus, Chick-fil-A's numbers are almost two times higher than those of McDonald's. By honoring the Lord, glorifying Him, putting Him first, and aligning itself with Biblical principles, Chick-fil-A's business is blessed.

"Sure, Rob, everyone knows that Chick-fil-A is the 'the Lord's chicken.' You can't compare their business to mine." This is the typical response I get when I point out these virtues. Okay then, let's take a look at a couple of companies in different fields that don't have the blessing of being the Lord's chicken to see if we can find other companies with similar blessings.

The second company that I would like for us to look at is Hobby Lobby. Hobby Lobby is committed to:

- Honoring the Lord in all we do by operating the company in a manner consistent with Biblical principles
- Offering customers exceptional selection and value
- Serving our employees and their families by establishing a work environment and company policies that build character, strengthen individuals and nurture families
- Providing a return on the family's investment, sharing the Lord's blessings with our employees and investing in our community

All Hobby Lobby stores are closed on Sundays. Here is their story:

In 1970, David and Barbara Green took out a $600 loan to begin making miniature picture frames out of their home. Two years later, the fledgling enterprise opened a 300-square-foot store in Oklahoma City, and Hobby Lobby was born. Today, with more than 900 stores, Hobby Lobby is the largest privately owned arts-and-crafts retailer in the world with over 43,000 employees and operating in 48 states.[5]

The Greens, like the Cathys, realized that by aligning their goals with God's goals, their company would be blessed. They have a partner on their side, and they have been richly rewarded. Let's compare Hobby Lobby with Michaels, the largest arts-and-craft store:

Michaels
- Revenue (2020): $5.271 billion
- Stores: 1,252
- Average Annual Store Revenue: $4,210,063
- Open 362 days a year (closed Christmas, Thanksgiving, and Easter Sunday)
- Average Daily Revenue per Store: $11,630

Hobby Lobby
- Revenue (2020): $4.6 billion
- Stores: 932
- Average Annual Store Revenue: $4,935,622
- Open 312 days a year (closed Sundays and Christmas)
- Average Daily Revenue per Store: $15,819

Comparing these two, we see that Michaels is open fifty-three more days per year, operating their business 15

---

5. "Our Story," *Hobby Lobby Newsroom*, accessed December 6, 2023, newsroom.hobbylobby.com/corporate background.

percent more than Hobby Lobby. Hobby Lobby's per-store revenue is 17 percent higher than that of Michaels. Hobby Lobby's daily revenue is 36 percent higher than Michaels.

This is the result of Hobby Lobby aligning their values and goals with God's. Once again, we see that Hobby Lobby, although being open 15 percent less than their competition, had per-store daily revenue that was 36 percent higher. God provides for them in six days more than their competitor does in seven days. Allen F. Morgenstern is credited with a saying dating back to the 1930s, when he developed a simplification program to increase productivity. As an industrial engineer, he coined the phrase, "Work smarter, not harder." From what we have read above, we clearly learn that God's way is the smart way.

Lastly, the most incredible story that shows faithfulness to stand strong in the face of adversity is that of Correct Craft. The outside pressure to perform and responsibility that they had on them was incredible, with the fate of the world in their hands. Instead of acting out of stress, they stood steadfast in the Lord, and as a result have an incredible testimony, as told on their site. Bill Yeargin, President and CEO of Correct Craft, describes the rich history and faith culture of his company. Correct Craft, which builds Nautique boats, was founded by the Meloon family with this mission statement: "To build boats to the glory of God." Along with many faith initiatives, they first strive to live in such a manner that employees who may never go to church come to Christ.[6]

During World War II, the company (along with several other companies) was assigned by the U.S. government to

---

6. "Who We Are," Correct Craft, accessed December 6, 2023, correctcraft.com/who-we-are/.

B.B.B. (Building Business Biblically)

build more than four hundred boats in thirty days. This meant Correct Craft was expected to work on Sundays. Despite the pressure and huge output expected of them, the company stayed true to their no-work-on-Sabbath commitment and succeeded in making the deadline. Meanwhile, the other companies with the same task worked Sundays but fell short of the goal. From then on, the company was famous for both its work excellence and commitment to faith culture. *National Geographic* dubbed Correct Craft's unique production process as a "Miracle Production," solidifying their reputation for having a faith culture.[7]

All these companies partner with God. They put Him first, and they honor our Father in everything they do. I practice this same belief system and have put it into effect across all businesses that I have owned and operated. By putting God first and honoring our Father, I have been blessed. I made the commitment from day one to be closed on the weekends. I observe the Sabbath, I put God first, and I appreciate my employees' time for God, worship, and their families.

My story isn't as monumental as that of Correct Craft such that my business changed the course of war, but nonetheless, it stands out from the rest. My business is located in a small-town market in a city not many have heard of. My team and I built this company in a down economy in the wake of the Great Recession of 2008. While many businesses and families were struggling to keep their doors open, our company flourished. Focused on treating our employees and customers right while adhering to the values of putting the Lord our God first, we not only survived but thrived through this time.

---

7. "The Correct Craft Story," Correct Craft, accessed December 6, 2023, correct-craft.com/history/.

We entered a global pandemic that created fear and havoc across the globe—something that was never seen before. During this time, we increased our year-over-year (YOY) sales and kept all our employees employed. We focused on honoring God with our hard work. We honored God by putting Him first, and He made the impossible possible. Just like Correct Craft, we stood faithful in our belief that by putting the Lord our God first, He would provide for us.

The result for me was that I was able to sell my business to a Fortune 500 company, freeing me up to pursue my passion of sharing my story with the world in hopes of helping other business owners position their companies in the same manner. Standing faithfully just as in Exodus, our God will fulfill the promise He has for us.

- Matthew 19:26: "Jesus looked at them and said, 'With man this is impossible, but with God all things are possible.'"
- Luke 18:27: "Jesus replied, 'What is impossible with man is possible with God.'"
- Matthew 17:20: "He replied, 'Because you have so little faith. Truly I tell you, if you have faith as small as a mustard seed, you can say to this mountain, "Move from here to there," and it will move. Nothing will be impossible for you.'"

CHAPTER 7

EMBRACE THE SUCK

Each time I write a book, I have a chapter in my head when I am outlining the book that I can't wait to get to. This is that chapter. The information that I run through in this chapter, if learned, utilized, and applied, will be life-changing to you and your business. But remember, there is always a *but*. Lance Armstrong, as we all know, had some struggles in his life. He went from the top of his game to the top of a doping scandal that rocked all of sports. But regardless of what he did, these words of his are still true: "Pain is temporary. It may last a minute, or an hour, or a day, or a year, but eventually it will subside and something else will take its place. If I quit, however, it lasts forever."

How many times in our daily lives do we face things that are challenging—things that cause us pain? This pain is where the win occurs. Without the pain, without the headache, without putting in the work, there is no reward. Our society has become so accustomed to easy, quick, immediate results. Technology has taken away the work needed to actually do most everything in our day-to-day lives. The drug industry has taken away the need for any aches and pains. All of this technological and medical advancement has moved us forward in so many areas, but not in the areas that build up mental toughness or determination. Thinking back over the last twenty to thirty years, we have put technology in place to take away conflicts and uncomfortable situations. By eliminating pain—making things easier or better—we have the expectation that things will always be faster, more efficient, better, and as a result, easier.

The side effect of this is that by eliminating pitfalls and challenges to our lives and not going through them or learning to embrace them, our minds and bodies don't have the training or perseverance to face and overcome challenges. Anyone who has done manual labor or even worked in the yard for a day knows the struggle. Grab a shovel, start working. More than likely, by the end of the day, your hands will have blisters on them from the work being done. But grab the shovel the next day and do the same thing—then the next day and the one after that. Over time, your hands will transition from soft and tender baby hands to calloused, tough hands. These callouses on your hands are what we need for our minds.

Lance Armstrong isn't the only one who knows this to be true. If we go to the Bible, 2 Chronicles 15:7 says: "But as for you, be strong and do not give up, for your work will be rewarded." Your work will be rewarded. You see, the Bible teaches you what you should be doing. To be rewarded, you have to put in work. The pain that you go through is what creates the breakthrough or the value. But the only way to get the breakthrough is to go through what I call the suck, meaning the pain that comes from challenges, struggles, hard work, and sometimes even failure.

You see, the goal can't be to eliminate the suck. If we eliminate the suck, then we no longer have the feeling of success. Everything is a win. Without the suck, how do we know the good? If everything we do in our day is easy and we don't know the agony of defeat, how do we feel the joy of winning? We can't experience the joy and the emotional stimulation of a win without also going through the emotions of loss. These defeats are what build up the callouses of our mind, body, and soul. The losses are what drive us to put in the hard work—to outwork the competition and to push through the hard times.

Now, people hear the word *competition* and think, "Where I'm from, everyone gets a trophy." When everyone gets a trophy, no one wins (and by the way, this is not good for kids). One article clearly defines this misconception:

> A winner or loser effect exists *only* if the fitness gain of the beta individual in a hierarchy, relative to that of the alpha, is less than 0.5. Then a loser effect *can* exist alone, or it can coexist with a winner effect; *however* [drum roll please], there cannot exist a winner effect without a loser effect.[1]

Without a loser, there can be no winner. It's impossible by definition. We can't eliminate the losses. We can't cut out the struggles and the hard times. These are what build us up, what drive us, and what create the callouses in our lives.

---

1. M. Mesterton-Gibbons, "On the Evolution of Pure Winner and Loser Effects: A Game-Theoretic Model," *Bull. Math. Biol.* 61 (November 1999): 1151–86, doi.org/10.1006/bulm.1999.0137.

One definition of *competition* according to *Oxford Languages* is: "interaction between organisms, populations, or species, in which birth, growth and death depend on gaining a share of a limited environmental resource."[2] There will always be a winner and a loser even if it's only you. Will you win or will you lose to the challenge? You tell yourself you are going to run a mile, and you stop at .99. You lost. You didn't hit your goal. No one else knows. My seventh-grade gym teacher used to tell us that's like peeing in the shower. You're not hurting anyone but yourself.

Don't let yourself get beat. Stay in the suck. Win the challenge—the competition—and see it through to the other side. This also shows you while you are going through the suck that there will be victory. There will be a win. There will be an end to your current struggle. Your feelings toward your challenge can change and push you to stay in until you get through it.

So, let's circle back now to technology and how technology has made it harder to live in the suck. Example one. Dating. Anyone that was born before 1990 has probably gone through the typical, what I will call old-fashioned dating. During the '80s and '90s, it was typically a man and a woman dating, which makes this example so much easier. A guy would have to approach a girl in person, use actual words, articulating himself in such a way that she remained interested in him, and then proceed to have an engaging conversation to generate interest from the female.

For most, the desired result was not optimal on the first try. I read somewhere that 97 percent of all pickup attempts failed. With a 97 percent failure rate, why did guys continue

---

2. *Oxford Languages*, s.v. "competition (*n.*)," accessed December 8, 2023.

to do it? A 97 percent chance of getting denied, turned down, failure? Why even try? Because they knew that through all the pain, the reward was on the other side—that although there was a 97 percent chance of failure, the perseverance of pushing through it would lead them eventually to the desired result. It might take one conversation or a thousand conversations, but they knew that they had a 3 percent success rate and that if they kept on trying, they would eventually break through and succeed at beating the suck phase.

Now, you might think that this is a silly example, and what does this have to do with your business? The correlation is that everything that we do in life builds character traits that we use in other parts of life. Those that are willing to put forth hard effort in one aspect of their lives typically have the same mindset in other aspects of their life. The habits that you create for yourself define you and become part of your DNA.

In comes technology, with the goal of making life easier. Now, instead of approaching the pretty girl that you see when you are actually outside your home, you send her a message from behind your computer. You can copy and paste your pickup line and send it out to a hundred girls in less time than it would have taken you to put pants on, make yourself presentable, climb up out of your mom's basement, and actually go talk to a real girl. Technology has eliminated the downside. You have a very small chance of disappointment because you're in the safety of your own home, hiding behind a screen covered in Doritos dust with a hot pocket sticking out of your mouth. You no longer need to put in any effort—you've eliminated the suck. But by eliminating the suck—the work it takes to break through for the victory—you eliminate the success on the other side, and you don't get the breakthrough.

Hence, increased divorce. In the 1950s, if you had a divorce, you had to go back out into society and try to find a new partner and go through that tough cycle all over again. Now, you just reactivate your online-wife marketing campaign. As in the Staples commercial, you now have an "easy button." But with every easy button, you lose something, and you take something away from your life. You lose the benefit of overcoming the struggle.

Remember, when you look back at your life—on how you made it to where you are now—it is where you came from that made you who you are. This work—this suck—is what created who you are. Do you embrace the suck, do you dig deep in the challenge, do you look forward to grinding it out and building the callouses of your life so that when an obstacle comes your way you yawn and say, "That ain't squat"? Or do you wake up looking at the metaphoric speed bump in front of you and think, "How am I going to overcome this mountain in my life?" Proverbs 27:17 (NKJV) says: "As iron sharpens iron, so a man sharpens the countenance of his friend." The struggles that we go through, the issues that we overcome, and the victory on the other side will never be as sweet or as satisfying without first going through the struggles.

All this brings us to the real question of this chapter. How do we overcome these struggles? How do we stay in the suck and keep our minds right to enable us to see victory on the other side? This is actually much simpler than most think. In order to get our minds right, we have to first set a goal. This goal can be anything from increasing sales, improving profits, or improving efficiencies to scaling our business.

Once you have the goal, the second step is to track the goal. More is more when it comes to tracking. The more you track, the more successful you will be. In tracking your KPI's, you can use any measure of progress that pertains to your goal. If you are trying to increase sales, then track each and every lead, call, contact, and the result of each interaction. What went right and wrong with each interaction? What could have been done differently? How can you tweak the process? How can you improve the results? Without tracking the information day to day, week to week, month to month, and year to year, you will not know the actual success rate of the work you are putting in or even if the work you are putting in is productive.

Thirdly, to help keep your mind focused on the goal, you take your original goal and set up mini goals. If you stick with sales, like the example in chapter 6, then you can't reach $1,000,000 in sales without first reaching $10,000, $50,000, and $100,000 in sales. So, you set these smaller mini goals to give yourself a sense of small wins along the way to your actual goal. These small wins help keep you focused on your goal. They keep the excitement in place.

Fourth, with the completion of each of these mini goals, you then set up a reward system to allow you to celebrate these victories. Now, this doesn't have to be anything crazy, but it does need to be something that shows you that the work is worth it and that you can do what you set out to do.

In his book *The Gap and the Gain*, author Dr. Benjamin Hardy discusses the vision of goals being like the horizon. We can see the horizon clear as day—it's out there—but no matter what we do, we can't get any closer to it. The horizon moves, and our goals move as we make progress toward the goal. This is why it's so important to have clear goals and mini goals so that we keep our original goal in focus and work toward accomplishing this goal and rewarding ourselves for the successes along the way.

Step five is accountability. From my experience, this seems to be the hardest step for most. *Accountability* seems to be a forgotten word in the society that we live in today. By definition, *accountability* is "the fact or condition of being accountable; responsibility."[3] How this translates into life is that you take ownership of the goals and the commitments that you make. This is where the rubber hits the road. Up until this point, it has been easy. Anyone can wake up and make a goal, set some mini goals, set up a plan to track their goals, and come up with rewards for themselves for doing a good job. All these things are feel-good items. But remember, there is always a *but*. Having the mental capacity to hold yourself directly accountable for your success or failure in meeting your goals is what separates those that do from those that don't.

This is where you embrace the suck. You can't punt the suck phase down the road. You can come up with excuses about how outside things prevented you from doing what you needed to do, or you can make any number of excuses along the way as to why you might have had issues hitting the goals you set. But the only thing that matters and the only thing you need to look at is your accountability. Either you were accountable to yourself and were successful, or you let yourself down and failed. Those are the only two outcomes. These are the only two choices you can make: do you respect yourself enough to live up to the expectations that your previous self set, or will you let yourself down by justifying your failure to accomplish your goal or blaming it on some outside force?

---

3. Ibid., s.v. "accountability (*n.*)," accessed December 8, 2023.

This is where books, coaches, friends, family, etc., can only do so much. If you can't stay in the suck for the minute, the hour, the day, or the week, then you don't deserve the win. In an age of everyone getting a trophy, no one wants to take accountability. In life, there are winners and there are losers. The winners are those that have figured out how to set goals, work toward those goals, and develop ways to hold themselves accountable for those goals to be successful. The others—the ones that expect the trophy for losing—haven't developed the mental fortitude or attitude to hold themselves to these higher standards. If you are honest with yourself, then I'm sure deep down, you will agree.

I don't know a single story about someone that made their mark on this world who gave up, didn't outwork others, didn't win, or didn't excel in their field or their craft. No one cares why you didn't meet a goal. No one cares why you weren't able to do something. We all have issues. We all have obstacles, and we all have problems. No one wants you to make your problem theirs. It's time to put your (big-boy or -girl) pants on and take responsibility. If you want it, you can make it happen. If you don't make it happen, it's because you gave up too early or didn't work hard enough to become successful in what you wanted. It's truly that simple.

So, how did we end up at a point where society started rewarding mediocrity and failures? Think back to the caveman. If he stops pursuing the brontosaurus because it gets hard, he won't eat a brontosaurus burger for dinner. He will starve. What better motivation to keep on pursuing than not starving? This brings us to step six: embrace the struggle. The struggle creates the reward. As technology makes things easier, societal pressures allow for these failures to be rewarded.

This has long-term effects on everyone, teaching you that it doesn't matter how hard you work, it doesn't matter if you win or you lose, it doesn't matter if you sacrifice or not—you will still be taken care of. Just have fun.

This is what our government, the media, our schools, and our recreational programs are programming us from early childhood to accept—that this is a normal way of life. With this mindset and way of living, we won't go through the disappointments of failing and building up the tenacity that we will need to be the future entrepreneurs and business leaders of our generations. Not winning should push us harder to win—to go out and give it our all next time in hopes of a different outcome—a win. By having the comfort of either not keeping score, everyone getting a trophy, lowering the grade standards in school, or spreading the lie that it is possible for everyone to win, we discourage effort. Why try hard when I'm going to get a trophy anyway?

This lackadaisical attitude can be seen in our youth today. Applications for entry-level and service-industry jobs are at an all-time low. Young adults are remaining dependent on their parents longer and longer. According to Parents.com, 60 percent of parents say they provide financial help to their young-adult children aged eighteen to twenty-nine.[4]

This generation can't take care of themselves, and the mental state of our kids and young adults has never been lower. By making life easier using technology, we are actually programming their brains not to think and to expect an easy option, without effort or pain, for the hard parts of life. We

---

4. Kristi Pahr, "Why Kids Are Moving Out Later and How Parents Can Deal," November 7, 2019, *Parents*, parents.com/kids/teens/when-should-kids-move-out-of-their-parents-house/.

are robbing them of the ability to work through difficult times, problems, and disappointments to make themselves stronger, brighter, and happier with the win after the hard work. We are eliminating the defeat that builds the callouses. We are creating a society of young people that can't handle disappointment or don't have the ability to overcome obstacles for the victory right in front of them.

When we hinder young people from developing the ability to find and fight through to find their own way, the results are shocking. Their mental state is plummeting. Society is experiencing a rise in suicide and depression. This isn't a coincidence. If you hand a generation an easy button and they have no way of dealing with any struggle or disappointment, then their minds don't develop to be able to work through these problems. Without the ability to work through their problems, they fall into despair, depression, and even worse—suicide.

As humans, we need to have struggle, we need to have work, and we need to work through problems. It's how we are wired, it's how we are programmed, and it's how God created us to look for and depend on Him. We are not meant to have solutions through technology and society. We were created to seek God for the answers when we are in despair and going through struggles.

> Be strong and of good courage, do not fear nor be afraid of them; for the LORD your God, He *is* the One who goes with you. He will not leave you nor forsake you. (Deuteronomy 31:6 NKJV)

> Consider it pure joy, my brothers and sisters, whenever you face trials of many kinds, because you know that the testing of your faith produces perseverance. Let perseverance finish its work so that you may be mature and complete, not lacking anything. If any of you lacks wisdom, you should ask God, who gives generously to all without finding fault, and it will be given to you. But when you ask, you must believe and not doubt, because the one who doubts is like a wave of the sea, blown and tossed by the wind. That person should not expect to receive anything from the Lord. Such a person is double-minded and unstable in all they do. (James 1:2–8)

Working though the suck—the hard times—and taking the responsibility for our failures along the way, all while looking to Jesus to get us through these struggles, are what bring us through. When we ask, we "must believe and not doubt." To believe and not doubt, we have to have our minds right. We have to have the faith and fortitude to know that whatever we come across, we are going to fight through, and that when we ask God to stand with us, He will. God will bring us through the tough times. We must own this, believe it, have faith in it, and be determined to get through it. If we do this, we will succeed. As Christians, we are not meant to blend into society. We are meant to be lighthouses that shine brightly and warn others of the dangers that we see.

Do not conform, do not fall into the societal traps, and do not give up. Through the course of each and every day and in every decision you face in every situation, you have at least two options. You face a crossroads at each and every decision you make. You either have the choice to do or not to do—to do this or to do that. You have the choice of getting up in the morning when the alarm sounds, or you can hit snooze. You can go to the gym, or you can sit on the couch. The path of life isn't paved ahead of you—you pave it each and every day with the choices that you make, and you live by the actions that you take and the decisions that you make.

The cow, to illustrate, will sense a storm coming and will run with all her heart away from the storm. The cow, being what the cow is, can't outrun the storm due to her relatively slow speed and hence does not avoid the storm but prolongs the exposure to the storm by running with the storm—in its path, in the same direction of the pain that she was actually trying to avoid.

The buffalo, on the contrary, though biologically similar to the cow, approaches things in a very different manner. The buffalo also senses the storm, but the difference is that instead of turning and running away from the storm, the buffalo will run headlong into the storm. By running headlong into the storm, the buffalo actually reduces the pain and suffering and time that it is exposed to the storm.

By facing the storm, or problem, head-on, the buffalo reduces its exposure to the storm, the suffering it will go though, and the total amount of pain felt because of the storm. In both situations, it wasn't a question of whether or not these animals could avoid the storm. The storm was coming, and as in life, when the storm comes, there isn't much you can do. The only thing that you can do is change your mindset or how you react to the storm when you are faced with it. Like the storm chaser heading into the direction of the hurricane, the buffalo mindset is to deal with the storm head-on.

Do not fear or run. Do not cower or stand down, but face the situation with confidence and address the situation directly. Oftentimes, those with debt spend all their time avoiding paying bills. Those with personal or marriage problems avoid the much-needed conversation with their significant other or spouse. Maybe your situation is a bad boss or a dead-end job, but not addressing the situation only prolongs the pain and suffering of living your life in fear. Maybe you are living with the pain of a body that is overweight and out of shape, but the consequences of your unhealthy condition seem easier to deal with than the pain of waking up and working out.

We all have storms we are dealing with in life. But what if instead of running from them, we made a plan to turn around and run straight at them, addressing them directly? Instead of avoiding and running, what if we made the call we were avoiding, or we had the meeting that we dreaded, or we quit the job that was causing darkness and depression in our lives? What if instead of living in this fear, we did something about the situation we were fearing?

Luke 8:22–25 (AMP) in the Bible relates the story of a storm that Jesus and the disciples went through. Jesus was preaching on the shore of the Sea of Galilee and wanted to get away from the crowds on the shores, so He asked His disciples to take Him to the other side of the sea.

> Now on one of those days Jesus and His disciples got into a boat, and He said to them, "Let us cross over to the other side of the lake (Sea of Galilee)." So they set out. But as they were sailing, He fell asleep. And a fierce gale of wind swept down [as if through a wind

tunnel] on the lake, and they began to be swamped, and were in great danger. They came to Jesus and woke Him, saying, "Master, Master, we are about to die!" He got up and rebuked the wind and the raging, violent waves, and they ceased, and it became calm [a perfect peacefulness]. And He said to them, "Where is your faith [your confidence in Me]?" They were afraid and astonished, saying to one another, "Who then is this, that He commands even the winds and the sea, and they obey Him?"

CHAPTER 8

THERE IS NO SUCH THING AS A SHORT-TERM PLAN

Traditional business planning will have a business owner set up short- and long-term goals to establish an immediate action plan and a plan for the future. In theory it sounds correct. It allows you to focus your attention on the short-term (pressing) goals while setting a different target and a different objective for the long-term goals. This is where confusion sets in. In setting both a short- and a long-term plan, the goals don't always align. When we look at the success rates and the longevity of companies, the companies with successful track records have a clearly defined long-term goal that is included in all the areas of short-term, day-to-day operations.

This is where you create your commandments—your non-negotiables for your business. These are the rules, the foundation, the backbone, and the values that your business is founded on. These are the words that you paint on your walls and look for and instill in each and every employee that you hire. You teach them to your employees, they are the basis of your training manuals, and they are the traits you look for when interviewing candidates to join your team. These are your hard-stop, do-not-pass-go, do-not-collect-two-hundred-dollars nonnegotiables. Once you have them, they are not to be changed, and all decisions that you, your managers, and your employees make and your customers expect will align with them. Hard stop. That's it. They never change, they never waiver, and you never bend to temptation to allow these rules to be broken. These are the fundamentals for the longevity of your business.

Let me break this down with an example. As a business owner, your days can be bombarded with hundreds of decisions that need to be made in real time. As the owner, what will you use for your compass? Will it be your short-term plan or your long-term plan? What's the difference? you might be asking. In reality, the difference between these two objectives can be astronomical. If your short-term plan is meeting payroll on Friday, what corners could you cut in quality to get your project done early? If your compass is your short-term goal, then your perspective—your finish line—is meeting the short-term need of the business. This goal may or may not be aligned with your long-term objective.

About this temptation to cut corners, I hear, "Rob, it's only one time." Or, "I have to meet the short-term goals to stay in business for the long-term goals." Or, "Once I reach X, I'll do it the right way." Or, "My competitors don't do it like that." All of these excuses are just that: excuses to take shortcuts and to get focused on the short-term goal at hand while losing sight of the true objective. You have to think of your business as a marathon. Each step you take isn't to get through that step—it's to get you one step closer to the goal in the race. If you focus on the short-term goals, you might sprint ahead and win the mile. You might be first off the starting blocks. But if you don't stay focused on the end goal—if you don't set out and keep your mindset on the long-term goals and vision of the company—you might not make it to the finish line.

This is why I preach that all goals for your business have to be long-term goals. In each decision, you must have in mind your list of commandments that you are not willing to waiver on. Once you have your list of commandments, then you have to run every decision through this list to make sure that your decisions align with those goals. In the example above, if your goal is to be a five-star-rated contractor, then you can't cut corners on your project to get it completed to collect a check. Once you receive a bad review, your five-star rating will be gone. Once you compromise on your long-term goals, things can start to come unglued. Issues will come up. The temptation will always be there, but you have to be resolute and follow through on your nonnegotiables. Hebrews 10:23 tells us, "Let us hold unswervingly to the hope we profess, for He who promised is faithful." And just as God is faithful to us, we must be faithful to our foundational principles.

CHAPTER 9

GIVING

The tithe is for protection, the offering is for production.
—Author unknown

The importance of giving back passes by many in the pursuit of business success. With that in mind, I try to include a chapter in every book to show the importance of giving and how this powerful tool is not a burden but a blessing to your business and personal finances. As business owners especially, the idea of giving, receiving, and partnering with God is more relatable than explaining the concept and the value of it to non-business owners. In many of your businesses, you have partners. All these partners have a job in the business, they all bring different skill sets, they all bring different values, and they all work toward the common goal of the company.

We can understand this by looking at the quasi-partnership we all have with the government. This partnership allows us to be in business in this country. In America, this partnership means that the government is our partner in the form of taxation. In the U.S., the corporate tax rate is 21 percent—meaning every dollar our businesses make, the government is entitled to 21 percent of it. In this book, I'm not going to expand on the value of this tax or what this partnership brings to the table, to keep from skewing the point of the message, but for a baseline, realize that the government will be with us for the duration of our businesses, and they will want their 21 percent cut. Then, in addition to these corporate taxes, the government (our silent partner) will require self-employment taxes to cover Social Security and Medicare, in the amount of 15.3 percent, bringing Uncle Sam's piece of the pie to 36.3 percent.

So, it's natural to ask the questions, How can I give? What is giving? Why do I need to give? How can I get ahead when I'm giving 10 percent of whatever I make? I can barely make it on my current income—how am I supposed to tithe? How can I help others when I can barely help myself? All of these are valid questions.

When we live in the natural, it is understandable that fear of scarcity will arise. Fear is not of God, though. In all things in life, there are always two powers at play in each and every decision we make. Once we understand this, then we simply run each decision through what we know and make the rational decision based on that info. These two factors are scarcity and abundance. According to the Bible:

> Remember this: Whoever sows sparingly will also reap sparingly, and whoever sows generously will also reap generously. Each of you should give what you have decided in your heart to give, not reluctantly or under compulsion, for God loves a cheerful giver. And God

is able to bless you abundantly, so that in all things at all times, having all that you need, you will abound in every good work. (2 Corinthians 9:6–8)

This is where the paradigm shift has to occur in your mind. Your mindset needs to be that the blessing this partnership with God has for your business is so great that you are excited to see how it unfolds. As you sow (or give), it will also be given back to you. This is a powerful verse in the Bible. What kinds of blessings do you want to flow over your family and your business? Scripture says that God wants a cheerful giver—one that is happy to give to others, not one that feels like giving is a burden or a chore. The cheerful givers will be rewarded, and blessings will flow back to them. The Bible says God will "bless you abundantly" and that you will "reap generously." With this then, we need to break down a plan for giving and how to get your business aligned with God's promise.

The Bible talks about a "tithe." The tithe is a portion (10 percent) of your income given as an offering to your local church.

- Proverbs 3:9: "Honor the Lord with your wealth, with the firstfruits of all your crops."
- Leviticus 27:30 (TLB): "A tenth of the produce of the land, whether grain or fruit, is the Lord's, and is holy."

What these verses are saying is to give a portion (specifically a tenth) of whatever you make back to God. And firstfruits are the Bible's way of saying that you should give before you do anything else with your money rather than giving the leftovers. The word *tithe* literally translates to "tenth" in Hebrew. In the Hebrew Bible, it is a "mitzvah," or "Biblical requirement" to give the priest 10 percent of produce or production. In Hebrew, this is the *terumat hammaaser* ("a tenth offering"). If we look into the Greek translation, the most common word used for this is *dekate*, which means "a tenth part." If we dig in even deeper and look at the *King James Dictionary* of the Bible, the definition of *tithe* is:

> TITHE, *n.* The tenth part of any thing; but appropriately, the tenth part of the increase annually arising from the profits of land and stock, allotted to the clergy for their support. Tithes are personal, predial, or mixed; personal, when accruing from labor, art, trade and navigation; predial, when issuing from the earth, as hay, wood and fruit; and mixed, when accruing from beasts, which are fed from the ground.
>
> TITHE, *v.t.* To levy a tenth part on; to tax to the amount of a tenth.
>
> When thou hast made an end of tithing all the tithes of thine increase. Deut. 26.
>
> Ye tithe mint and rue. Luke 11.
>
> TITHE, *v.i.* To pay tithes.[1]

With this, we have our plan—our number, our giving, our tithe that is God's—that we will set aside and give back to God.

> "I the LORD do not change. So you, the descendants of Jacob, are not destroyed. Ever since the time of your ancestors you have turned away from My decrees and have

---

1. *KJV Dictionary*, s.v. "tithe (*n.*, *v.*)," accessed December 11, 2023.

not kept them. Return to Me, and I will return to you," says the Lord Almighty.

"But you ask, 'How are we to return?'"

"Will a mere mortal rob God? Yet you rob Me."

"But you ask, 'How are we robbing You?'"

"In tithes and offerings. You are under a curse—your whole nation—because you are robbing Me. Bring the whole tithe into the storehouse, that there may be food in My house. Test Me in this," says the Lord Almighty, "and see if I will not throw open the floodgates of heaven and pour out so much blessing that there will not be room enough to store it. I will prevent pests from devouring your crops, and the vines in your fields will not drop their fruit before it is ripe," says the Lord Almighty. "Then all the nations will call you blessed, for yours will be a delightful land," says the Lord Almighty. (Malachi 3:6–12)

The passage from Malachi above shows us that God is not taking from us. We are simply giving him 10 percent of what is already His. If we believe as it's written in Scripture that all things are from God, then 100 percent of what you receive is already His. Partnering with God is Him allowing you to keep 90 percent of what He has given you.

In Mark 12:17 (NLT), Jesus is being tested by the Pharisees when they ask Him if it's right to pay taxes. Jesus says to them, "Give to Caesar what belongs to Caesar, and give to God what belongs to God." Jesus understood that the government would tax His people. He understood that they would mandate taxes to be paid, and you and I as business owners are still under this mandatory partnership today with every dollar that we make and every dollar our businesses produce.

The choice that we all have, though, is whether we want to align our businesses and partner with God—to have Him on our side and to give Him the glory and the recognition that all things are from Him and to honor our commitment to having Him in our businesses with His 10 percent.

In my life, I could not think of a better partner to have by my side. Having God as a partner, producing 100 percent of the result and only wanting 10 percent of the benefit, is a no-brainer to me. If you feel like you are doing it all yourself—if you feel like you're all alone—then it's time to partner with God. He is there for you. He wants to help you. He wants to bless your business. You just have to ask Him and commit to partnering with Him.

CHAPTER 10

GO WITH YOUR GUT (DECISION-MAKING)

Prayer is telephoning to God, and intuition is God telephoning to you.
—Florence Scovel Shinn

Never second-guess your gut. How many times have you had the twinge, the feeling, the question arise inside of you in a situation, a deal, a change, or a business opportunity that just didn't seem right? From the outside, it may have seemed like an incredible opportunity. I remember hundreds of times as a contractor that I would meet a person, have an engineer call, or come across a project that seemed like it was an amazing opportunity. But there was something that seemed just a little bit off. Maybe it was something that the customer said, maybe it was something that I saw on the site, or maybe it was nothing that I could even see or hear but just something that I knew was off.

Early on, I had an issue with listening to my gut. I would overthink and proceed with a plan even after a gut check. The younger me and a lot of business owners that I talk to feel like the gut check was more like a challenge to overcome to take advantage of an opportunity than a warning light that it wasn't the right opportunity for us. Looking back, I had a scarcity mindset. If I passed up this job, this customer, this opportunity, then there might not be another. I read my gut check as fear of missing out vs. a warning to hold steadfast for something that aligned with my plan. Time and time again, I would overcome this feeling with willpower and hard work, enduring a project that wasn't a blessing to me but a stressful, unpleasant experience that never panned out as the tremendous opportunity that I thought it might be.

Then, in 2015, I reached a point in business that many business owners hope to reach. I negotiated the sale of my construction company. This deal had all the details of a fairy-tale ending. The buyer was a large commercial contractor that wanted to get into residential construction. We had the processes in place, the reputation, and the skill set to fast-track their business in this space five to seven years ahead of where they would be if starting out a new division. The synergies were there. I had an exit strategy in place for myself, and I was able to structure the deal to keep all my employees on board in positions as good as or better than they had with my company.

But... There is always a *but*. My gut was wrecked. I chalked it up to nerves, trying to convince myself of the value of the opportunity. Was I just scared? Was I not confident in my own abilities? Wasn't this my safety net? Each day, I'd fight through it, chalking it up to stress, chalking it up to nerves, chalking it up to something wrong with me versus listening to my gut. I went through many sleepless nights, tossing and

Go with Your Gut (Decision-Making)

turning, playing out scenario after scenario in my head, and praying to God to tell me what the right thing was to do.

Then it finally clicked. I had been asking the right question, but I hadn't been listening for the answer. I had been listening for the answer that I wanted to hear and not the answer that God was giving me. Thinking back on this situation and these decisions *now*, they seem like a no-brainer. But when you are in the moment and you are in your own head, the decisions that you need to make—no matter how simple—may seem larger than climbing a mountain. This is what I felt like I was facing.

I felt desperate and was grasping at anything I could hold on to for the sale of my business. The buyers would ask for a concession, I would agree, and then they would change a term. I would agree, time after time the deal would tweak and change, and I would agree to it, living in a fear of losing out on this opportunity of a lifetime to sell my company.

And then, I gave it all to God. I remember lying in bed one night with tears in my eyes, not knowing what to do and hearing the words in my head, "I've already told you." It was just like the clarity I received that night when I started the roofing company. The clarity came to me that this wasn't a healthy way to live. I awoke the next morning feeling rested, empowered, excited, and with a feeling for a new plan in my life. Never had I realized that my gut was talking to me—that my gut was actually my internal check-engine light that would guide me through life if I would just stop and listen to it. I remember explaining the situation to a friend—that I felt like I had been living my life up to that point with navigation on while I was driving, yet I ignored the turn-by-turn directions. Somehow, someway, I had made it to a few destinations, but how many wrong turns had I made along the way? How many headaches, problems, issues, and stresses could I have avoided had I just listened to what God was telling me to do?

It was April 7, 2015, and I made a promise to myself that day that I would always go with my gut. My gut would override my head in every situation. I gave myself a mental checklist. If I felt the check in my gut, I would count one, two, three. If the feeling was still there, I would go with my gut. If it wasn't, then it wasn't a gut check. Sounds simple, right? I was stretched extremely thin at this time in life, and my mind, body, and soul were wrecked from the inside out. Where this decision would have been hard for most to follow through with or transition to, I had no mental capacity left and was stressed to my limit. Any change that I could make to help with decision-making in life was a welcome opportunity.

That afternoon as I headed to the closing table, everything changed. After years of fighting and not listening to my gut, I had enough—enough of the debilitating stomach cramps, the sleepless nights of stress, the restless weekends. My life was passing by as a blur, and I needed to make a change. At that moment, a sense of clarity came upon me. I had a calmness that I hadn't previously experienced. I counted one, two, three. The feeling was still there. I picked up my phone and called the attorney's office where the closing was scheduled.

"Joe, it's Rob. I'm not coming in."

"What do you mean, Rob? The buyers are here, the wire has been sent, and everything is done!"

"Joe, the deals not right, the deal keeps changing, it's not right for my employees, and it's not right for me. I'm sorry it's all done, but there's been too much change from the original

Go with Your Gut (Decision-Making)

deal to where we are now. I've just been strung along with the process when I should have punted a long time ago."

"Rob, this isn't going to be good. Are you sure you want to do this?"

"Joe, you can't change the terms of the deal that we agreed to and assume I'm going to just go along from a fear of missing out. I'm done."

That day, I walked out on what I thought was going to be the biggest life-changing experience of my professional career. What came after was a year-long legal battle with the buyers of my company. During this year, I second-guessed my gut almost daily. "Should I have just succumbed to the buyers' demands? Did I make the right decision? Am I the one that's in the wrong? Did I do wrong by God, my employees, and my family?" Every day that passed, I would find myself sitting and wondering—second-guessing decisions and actions that should have given me freedom and instead landed me in a legal battle.

But as each day passed and as these thoughts crept in, I stopped and listened. I counted one, two, three. Each time I second-guessed myself, I would bring it to God. My internal counting one, two, three became the way I was able to stop all the noise of the world and give it to God. Each day, it became easier, and each day, as the reassurance and peace came over me as I practiced bringing the things of the world to Him, it became easier. It became easier to trust my gut. It became easier to make the decision that gave me an instant calmness. It became a habit to bring all my decisions to Him and run everything through this process first vs. waiting for the stress and turmoil to pile up before asking God for help.

The buyer eventually dropped the lawsuit. He had no basis and was just trying to pressure me into closing the deal. He thought by making me spend a bunch of money on legal fees, he would pressure me to sell him the business on his terms. His scheme didn't work, and he eventually dropped the case when he realized I would fight it till the end.

What happened as a result of learning to listen to my gut is my efficiency increased. No longer did it take time to deliberate on decisions that needed to be made. It was as simple as one, two, three. I went with my gut. No longer did my mind live in turmoil, running scenarios over and over in my head about possible outcomes before making the decision. One, two, three—decision made. This realization—this peacefulness of knowing that God is truly there in every decision that I make—brought back my confidence. I learned that I could bring to Him first each decision, each step, and each part of my life and that He has time to help me with every decision, big and small, that I bring. I still practice this same technique today. I bring everything in life to the Lord. Every decision, every request, every problem, and every victory belongs to Him.

> Rejoice in the Lord always. I will say it again: Rejoice! Let your gentleness be evident to all. The Lord is near. Do not be anxious about anything, but in every situation, by prayer and petition, with thanksgiving, present your requests to God. And the peace of God, which transcends all understanding, will guard your hearts and your minds in Christ Jesus. (Philippians 4:4–7)

CHAPTER 11

CASH FLOW

As entrepreneurs, it's inevitable that you have heard of cash flow and at least to some degree understand the importance of it to any business's survival. Quotes on the subject by many famous people have been repeated across the world. These sayings flow around boardroom tables and even cross mainstream media and music:

- P. T. Barnum: "Money is a terrible master but an excellent servant."
- Sir Richard Branson: "Never take your eyes off the cash flow because it's the lifeblood of your business."
- Wu-Tang Clan: "Cash rules everything around me C.R.E.A.M get the money dollar dollar bill, yo."

And from the Bible:

- Proverbs 21:5: "The plans of the diligent lead to profit."
- Proverbs 13:11: "Dishonest money dwindles away, but whoever gathers money little by little makes it grow."

So, what makes cash flow so important to a business? To understand this, let's start at the beginning. *Cash flow* by definition, according to *Oxford Languages*, is "the total amount of money being transferred into and out of a business, especially as affecting liquidity."[1] (*Liquidity* is the available liquid assets of a company.) This means that cash received by your business is cash inflow, and cash spent by your business is cash outflow. This all can go onto a cash-flow statement that reports your company's use of cash during whatever time period is selected—i.e., you can track to see if you are bringing in more money than you are spending. Now that we know what cash flow is, we can break down the endless debate on how to manage it.

In an ideal world, your business would always have positive cash flow. This means that hourly, daily, weekly, monthly, and yearly activities would always create positive cash flow for your business—i.e., your business would take in more money than it pays out. In reality, though, your business will probably have ebbs and flows of cash coming in and cash going out—meaning that you might bring in fifty dollars today but need to send out one hundred dollars. This potential deficit is where the debate comes in regarding how you manage cash flow.

The obvious answer to many is to finance the difference. In business, this finance option can take many forms. For many, this means accessing a line of credit, taking on an SBA loan, credit cards, personal loans, home equity loans on a home, business partners, venture capital, issuing stock, selling bonds, or any other form of financing to increase the liquidity of the business. If you choose to take on debt, you increase liquidity (influx of cash to the business), but you also create a liability (the repayment of this debt) that will

---

1. *Oxford Languages*, s.v. "cash flow (*n.*)," accessed December 12, 2023.

affect future cash flow of your business moving forward. I.e., you solve the problem today in hopes that you won't be in this situation tomorrow and that your financial position will improve to offset and service the debt payment and future cash-flow needs. Basically, you take on debt today to get you through until tomorrow because you believe that tomorrow will bring more cash.

In theory, this is a great solution. This influx of cash allows for a business to run more easily. The stress of generating cash is reduced, and the up and downs of business activity are leveled out. But... There is always a *but* in business. The *but* is, What if things don't improve? What if the influx of cash only solves the problem of cash flow today, and the business doesn't bring in more cash tomorrow? Then your cash-flow demand increases once again, requiring another influx of cash that will once again put strain on future cash-flow requirements by adding two debt payments to the present needs that are not being met.

This is a slippery slope to go down. Will this influx from a loan help you grow your business's cash inflow enough to take on the additional cash outflow that will result from the payments required to service the debt? This is the question. Society promotes a financial ideology that asks the question, "How much will my payment be?" with the idea that the true cost and actual value of the product, service, or convenience comes second. I say convenience because this is truly what taking on debt as a business is. It's a convenience—the convenience of not making sure you manage your cash flow correctly so you can take the easy way out.

Is it easier to put in the extra work to make the extra sale or keep your business open later to ensure you bring in the cash flow required to service your business needs, or is it easier to take on debt? From the outside, it looks like debt is the easier option. It always does. It's become almost a rite of passage for a new business owner to start a company, and then it's, "I got my first credit card." "I got my first line of credit." "I got my first SBA loan." "I got my first [insert debt here]." In society, it feels like an accomplishment to take on debt. My company must be doing well because XYZ bank wants to "give" me money. In reality, though, by taking on debt you are taking on a partner that is going to have influence on your business and will always need to be paid first—before you pay yourself.

Let's take a peek in the Bible to see what it says about borrowing. "The rich rule over the poor, and the borrower is slave to the lender" (Proverbs 22:7). Wow! The borrower is slave to the lender. I think they probably left that out of the loan application, and I doubt the banker mentioned that part during their sales call.

So, let's test it. If you take on debt, do you become slave to the lender? It's an honest and fair question, one that should probably be tested. You as the business owner receive a sum of money. Your business benefits from the influx of cash. Now, what are your obligations as the business owner for this influx of cash moving forward? Monthly payments. Monthly payments to whom? The bank. What happens if you don't make these payments? The bank will take back whatever collateral you posted to take on this debt or will come after your business. So, who controls your business now? If you have a bad month, does the bank care, or will you still have to make your monthly payment to your master? If that big contract doesn't come through, does the bank care? If your key employee leaves, you get sick, your wife divorces you, or you get in a car accident, does the bank care? No, the answer is no. You will still have to serve your master and make your payments to them.

You have given up the freedom you were searching for in becoming a business owner for a little bit of easy. For a little bit of easy you have taken on the burden of bondage to your lender. You have taken on a partner that has the utmost control of your business. You have put that partner in front of yourself, your family, and God. This isn't what the Bible teaches.

> For the LORD your God will bless you as He has promised, and you will lend to many nations but will borrow from none. You will rule over many nations but none will rule over you. (Deuteronomy 15:6)

How will you rule over many nations if you give up ruling over your own business? It's time for you to take back control of your business. The business that will create freedom from society's norms and allow you to live free will only work if you don't fall into the societal traps. Debt is this trap, debt will control you, and debt will take control of your business, your family, and your life. Controlling your decisions, what you can do, and how you can do it, debt can spiral into a whirlwind effect that can put you out of business and financially ruin your family.

So, what are we supposed to do if what we learn in business school and from reading business books and watching our government's fiscal policies isn't correct? It's time to take your cues from a different source. As Christians, we all know that the Word of God is truth. He cannot lie, He is omniscient, He is omnipotent, and He is omnipresent. What does that mean? That means that the Word of God given to us through the Bible is the word, the truth, and the structure for how we are to live our lives. His omniscience means that His power is not a blind power. Everything that God does has an intelligent purpose, a definite goal, and a reason for our lives. His omnipresence means He is in every place at every moment. God is present, meaning that He is here with us, not absent from our lives. Anywhere we are, He is with us—in all places and in all situations. Lastly, God has omnipotence, meaning He is all-powerful. His Word is never without power, so when He speaks, all creation obeys Him. This is where sin steps in. Although God can control all things, He gives us free will. We have the ability to listen to what He says, or not. The choice is ours.

So, the real question then becomes, How do you avoid these societal traps while managing the cash flow of your business, and how do you align your business under the principles of the Bible to partner with God? This can be broken down into three simple steps to implement in your current or new business plan.

Step 1: Make God's Plan Your Plan

What this means is that God's plan will put you in the proper position and place based on what you can handle and what you are ready for at any particular time in life. He will not give you much if you are not ready, and He will not hold back from you if you are ready for more. It's easy to aspire to have your business mimic or resemble others that you see. It's easy to get caught up in planning your business growth based on others you see in the world. Many business owners see competitors and think, "I can be there next week, month, year if only I do [insert action here]." But whose plan are you following? Are you truly ready for everything that comes along with it? How do you know that the plan you are putting together for your life is the right plan? How do you know the business that you are trying to mimic will actually stay in business?

- Psalms 32:8 (AMP): "I will instruct you and teach you in the way you should go; I will counsel you [who are willing to learn] with My eye upon you."
- Jeremiah 29:11: "'For I know the plans I have for you,' declares the LORD, 'plans to prosper you and not to harm you, plans to give you hope and a future.'"
- Psalms 37:7 (NLT): "Be still in the presence of the LORD, and wait patiently for Him to act. Don't worry about evil people who prosper or fret about their wicked schemes."

In action, this alignment means reviewing your current business structure to see if your goals are reflective of God's and follow Biblical truths. If they don't, then chances are your plan isn't aligned properly. Take a look at your business plan, your mission statement, and your one-, two-, three-, and five-year goals. Do they align with the ways of the world, or the ways of God? Does your plan require taking on debt? Does your plan require unfair or unlawful business practices? Does your plan require you or your employees to sacrifice putting God and your families first? If you answered yes to any of these questions, then I urge you to rethink and realign your plan.

Step 2: A Plan for Your Plan

Now that you have reviewed your business plan and made any tweaks and changes necessary to align it with the Bible, it's time to actually implement the plan. If growth, expansion, hiring employees, opening up new locations, purchasing equipment, etc., are part of your plan, then you need to line item an actual plan to reach these goals. Yes, the easy button means going down to the local bank and applying for a loan—but remember, you are managing your cash differently, thinking backwards from your solution to your plan.

For example, your business needs to purchase a new $50,000 piece of equipment. You are able to afford $5,000 down, and let's say you have $1,500 per month of free cash flow. This allows you to set up a separate equipment account with your bank and QuickBooks to plan and save for this piece of equipment, allowing a full purchase of the equipment in thirty months. Without taking on debt, you now position yourself to become more profitable once you bring this equipment on board, and you do not increase your monthly cash-outflow requirements. If this equipment is something that is truly a priority of the business, then additional work, savings, and prioritization will be made to fund this account faster than the thirty months originally estimated.

On the other hand, if you take on debt, the scenario looks like this:

$50,000 purchase price
$5,000 down payment
10% interest
<u>$1,452 monthly payment</u>
Total Cost $56,272

You have instant access to the equipment, but you have locked yourself into payment terms for the next thirty-six months. What if the market turns? What if you were wrong and you didn't need the machine? What if the machine isn't able to increase production? You have locked yourself in for thirty-six months of payments and used up all available free cash flow for a piece of equipment that doesn't have the positive effect on your business that you hoped. Secondly, once you have payments for this machine, you no longer have the $1,500 a month in free cash flow to allocate to other ideas or opportunities that may arise.

Step 3: Make Your Own Payment Terms

My favorite saying in business is, "You can pick the price if I can pick the terms." This speaks to just how important terms can be in managing the cash flow of your business. If you don't agree with the quote above, I'll happily buy anything you're selling. Now, any business that has suppliers will undoubtedly have some sort of terms to pay them for the goods they provide. These initial terms stipulate how the suppliers want you as the customer to pay them back. Some terms allow for a net one, seven, thirty, forty-five, or sixty days to make the payment without paying any interest. Some offer a discount of 1, 2, or 5 percent to pay within a certain timeframe. As a business owner, you have to manage these terms to create the most value for your business. Do not blindly accept what the suppliers are offering. These terms can be negotiated, and just like cash flow is important to you, it is important to your vendors.

What does this look like in real life? In the course of operating my business, my team and I developed a tremendous relationship with a material supplier that we used almost exclusively. This was a large account, and we had a great relationship. Our terms from the vendor were 2% / 45 / net 60, meaning that we had forty-five days to pay the vendor in full to get a 2 percent discount on the materials that we were purchasing. If we couldn't do that, then we had an additional fifteen days to pay them before our account would incur interest, bringing us to net 60.

Traditional business-school fundamentals teach that you use OPM (other people's money), and with that you hold on to your cash as long as you can so that you can use it in your business vs. paying off accounts payable. But remember, we are not here to teach you the ways of Wharton. We are running our cash flow on the ways of Yahweh.

With that in mind, in a typical month, our average monthly spend was around $2,500,000 with this material supplier. This meant that we spent $625,000 for materials each and every week, meaning we had to produce and collect quickly to stay ahead of these numbers. To do that, I developed a system that allowed our business to use our vendor's accounts-payable terms to access funds as needed for capital expenditures that arose, or to manage cash flow if collection issues came up that would not allow for us to meet our payment terms.

Here is how it broke down: Our payment terms were forty-five days net, 2 percent, meaning that I was never going to make a payment to the vendor that was over forty-five days old because I needed that 2 percent profit for the bottom line of my business. That was free money—never turn your back on this. We took in $50,000 a month in rebates at this level, or $600,000 per year in discounts, just to pay our bills on time. Okay, I digressed—I just want everyone to see the power of not taking your eye off the little things—the details, the small items—that can add up to huge numbers.

Back to payment terms. I had forty-five days to hold on to my money, as Wharton teaches, to use for my business while my vendor was sitting there counting down the days for me to pay them. But that's exactly what I did *not* do, and this is what I want you to stop doing. My average turn cycle for the eleven years I ran finances for our company was twenty-one days. What that meant was that I had twenty-four days of slack on my payment cycle in case capital expenditures arose. Why? you might be asking yourself. By keeping my internal terms at twenty-one days vs. the vendor's allowed forty-five days, I freed up twenty-four days on my payment cycle to allow for "oh crap" in my business.

To break this down in dollar and cents, we know that we were running $2,500,000 in materials on a thirty-day cycle. This means that based on our terms, I was able to go to $3,750,000 ($2,500,000 per 30 days + $1,250,000 per 15 additional days of purchasing) without losing our discount and without hitting our fifteen-day zone of no discount before we were paying interest. This meant that every day I was prepaid ahead of the forty-five-day-net term date gave me access to $83,333 in cash. So, looking at my average turn cycle, I had in theory access to $83,333 x 24 days = $2,000,000 in free cash flow to use in my business.

Managing the payment terms ended up being the biggest financial blessing our business ever had. If we had cash needs for the business in a week, I could slide back my turn cycle to free up $83,000 per day to use toward the need. Then, as free cash came available again, I would pay back down to get our turn cycle back to twenty-one days. In explaining this process to the Fortune 500 company that eventually purchased our business, the new CFO was baffled. How was a company with $100,000,000 in gross annual sales operating without any debt or lines of credit? It was unheard of. I laid out this plan as I did above and explained to them the processes that we had in place built on the foundation that this was God's plan and that I was simply the steward of His plan moving forward.

Step 4: Multiple Accounts

In Step 2, I briefly touched on the multiple-account concept of managing cash flow. The multiple-account concept allows your business the flexibility to compartmentalize micro-goals. It allows you to set up, manage, and track progress to each goal in this underlying account, and it allows you to set up systems and KPIs to track the performance of each of the goals easily. This system also prevents goal haze, as I call it, that comes from holding all cash in the operating account. For my businesses, I kept a minimum of four accounts:

1. Operating account. This covers day-to-day operations and spending.

2. Owners' account. This account holds money intended for distributions to owners. I prefer to hold this in an interest-bearing money-market account.

3. Capital-expenditure account. This money-market account that earns interest holds funds needed to reach capital-expenditure requirements of the business at some

future time. This can be tools, equipment, expansion, etc.—any potential future larger purchase.

4. Savings account. This money-market account that earns interest holds funds (free cash) set aside from the business for future needs. This is different from a capital-expenditure account. This account may be drawn on in times of business slowdown, emergency, or when situations arise that were unforeseen. This account expects the unexpected. It levels out the ups and downs in your business cycles and ensures you have a safety cushion.

These four steps, if implemented properly in not only your business plan but also your business culture, will set your business apart and give you the resources necessary to weather any downturn, take advantage of any opportunity, and ensure the longevity of your business for generations to come. I close this chapter with a passage from Proverbs 3:13–18:

> Blessed are those who find wisdom, those who gain understanding, for she is more profitable than silver and yields better returns than gold. She is more precious than rubies; nothing you desire can compare with her. Long life is in her right hand; in her left hand are riches and honor. Her ways are pleasant ways, and all her paths are peace. She is a tree of life to those who take hold of her; those who hold her fast will be blessed.

CHAPTER 12

DEBT

The rich rule over the poor, and the borrower is slave to the lender.
(Proverbs 22:7)

While writing this, I debated leaving only the single passage of Scripture above as the entirety of chapter 12. I talked about this exact same Scripture in chapter 11 while going over cash flow, but the impact of it is so vast that I had to dig deeper into how it affects other aspects of business. This single sentence in the Bible formed my desire to dig deeper and deeper into Scripture to find the meaning and understanding of how God truly wants us to operate not only our businesses but also our personal finances.

When we break down these fourteen words, there is no question of how God is instructing us to live. The borrower is slave to the lender. When we take on debt, we make the conscious decision to trade our freedom for the money that someone or some entity is trying to give us. As business owners, we have to be aware of this. How many calls, advertisements, and offers do you receive from people trying to lend you money—credit-card offers in the mail, lines of credit, home-equity loans, billboards, text messages for additional capital, and business-financing requests when you go to the bank? I spent the last seven days tracking the number of interactions that I personally received that offered some type of financing. The results were shocking:

- Credit card offers in the mail: 7
- Text messages for business financing: 4
- Bank offers (in person and via email): 5
- Commercials (I don't watch much TV): 2
- Phone calls for financing needs: 8

You are bombarded with countless commercials and billboards for mortgages, refinancing, cash advances, low-interest car loans, and the list goes on and on. So, it bears asking why—why all the interest in offering you money? Why do all these people want so badly to "help you" buy a new [insert item here]?

I've never run across someone so interested in helping me, yet I also have never run across an advertisement that truly had my best interest in mind. The offer wasn't "too good to be true." The reality is that we use debt and financing as an easy button for our lives. It allows a fast-forward on our operations, our lives, and our wants to a future date vs. accepting the reality of where we are today in our finances.

You might be reading this now, saying, "My business needs to expand. We need a loan for expansion, location equipment, operating capital, etc." Do you, though? Do you *need* to take on debt to accomplish your goals, or is it the simpler option—the easy button, the magic pill—that allows you to take the easier way in life? I'd argue that you don't need the financing. If you want to expand, then you should be setting aside capital and resources from the current business operation to be able to meet the expansion needs of your business. Debt is a trap. Debt is simply the transfer of the freedom of one person to someone else.

For additional details, or if you would really like an eye-opening worldly view on this topic, I recommend you read *The New Confessions of an Economic Hit Man*, by John Perkins. At the time of this writing, it is available as a free download on Audible.

CHAPTER 13

MONDAY QUARTERBACK

Everyone has heard the expression "Monday quarterback" before. The premise is that it's super easy to say what a quarterback should have done during any particular play in a game once you know the outcome of that play. If the play results in a turnover, or they miss a wide-open receiver, fumble the ball, get sacked, or make a wrong call, it's very easy to judge and point out what they should have done differently. The same goes for business. It's easy to look from the outside in and say what you think the leaders of the organization should be doing differently. But knowing the inner workings of the company and seeing what the leaders themselves see while running the business opens up a whole different vision.

As entrepreneurs, we face a variety of difficulties on a day-to-day basis. Starting out, these can be our first sale, hiring employees, or managing cash, to name a few. What I have found, though, is that the most significant problems that we face are either our self-limitations or an aggrandized view of our talents. I.e., either we don't think that we are good enough, or we think that we are better than everyone else.

These two extremes can be equally harmful to our businesses. On one hand, if we don't have the confidence in our abilities to make the decisions needed to move the company forward, then our businesses can fail. And if we are too arrogant to look around, consult others, and take in information from them, that can also have a negative effect on our businesses.

Using the example of the quarterback above, the quarterback is looked upon as the leader on the field. This doesn't mean that he doesn't first seek guidance and direction from others to help him make the best decision. As the quarterback of your business, you have to reach out to others and allow them the opportunity to share what they see. Whose input is important in making your business decisions? Input can come from a variety of different people in your circle—coaches, CPAs, attorneys, employees, vendors, customers, suppliers, and even competitors. All these people see your business from a very different perspective from yours. They are also not as personally involved in your business as you, so they can see other perspectives or angles on the full picture while you may be focused on the micro.

The clinical diagnosis of this mental limitation, according to Cleveland Clinic, is visual agnosia: "This is where you can see the parts of an object but can't recognize the object itself. An example of this is identifying the wheels, seat, and handlebars of a bicycle when you look at each part, but you can't recognize them as part of the whole bicycle."[1] This can be common in business as well. You could be looking at your business and identifying an issue. Maybe you see the need for increased sales, so you increase marketing, add salespeople,

---

1. "Agnosia," Cleveland Clinic, accessed December 14, 2023, my.clevelandclinic.org/health/diseases/24463-agnosia.

and incentivize customers. Your focus is all on increasing the top dollar when the issue may not actually be sales. It could be profitability. Maybe you are stretched too thin on margin already, and that's why you need the increased sales. Maybe your current infrastructure can't handle the sales volume that you have, and it's inefficient. Maybe the sales that you are making are not profitable to your business, but since you're so close to the action you're not seeing the full picture. You see the handlebars, the seat, and the wheels, but you don't see the bicycle.

This is where we as entrepreneurs need the guidance and the input from those around us to fill in the missing parts and pieces. We can all make it to a certain point in our businesses on our own, relying 100 percent on our own abilities, our own virtues, and our own insights. But to break through to the next level, we need to ask the questions of others to fill in the missing pieces of the picture in our heads. If we don't, we can end up chasing the rabbit down the wrong hole. Sometimes, we catch our wrong turn in time. But other times, we keep doubling down, working harder, and spending more resources, time, manpower, and money to continue the chase in the wrong direction, only to find ourselves farther and farther away from the finish line and our very own plan.

An example of this is a construction company for which I did a business overview. This business, like many of those in the construction industry, was very heavily dependent on the owner's involvement. The processes and procedures in place seemed to work from the outside looking in but weren't getting the owner to his desired goal.

The basic premise that the owner saw was that by having a fuel account for vehicles at a certain discount store, he would save money on the discounted fuel. The reality of it, though, was that he created an unnecessary step in his business process that not only cost his business money but also reduced overall productivity, which resulted in a counterproductive step away from his business goals. Here is the perceived benefit versus the actual cost:

Summary
- 7% savings on fuel cost
- Average fuel fill-up: 25 gallons
- Fuel cost: $3.19/gallon at discount location
- Fuel cost: $3.41/gallon at non-discount retail location
- Average savings per fill-up: $.22/gallon, or $5.50/tank

Owner's Perceived Benefit
- Savings of $5.50 tank
- Weekly savings, based on two tanks/week: $11.00
- Yearly savings: $572.00 (104 tanks)

Hidden Costs
- 2 employees' time at average cost of $60/hour
- Additional distance to drive across town to discount location (7 miles from business location)
- Half gallon of fuel to get to discount location
- Drive time from office to discount location (15 minutes)
- Additional time at pumps (these discount pumps had additional wait time of approx. 17 minutes longer than retail location due to high demand)

Actual Cost
- Additional fuel use:

.5 gallons x 104 trips = 52 gallons of fuel @ $3.19/gallon: $165.88

- Additional labor:

15 + 17 minutes/trip = 32 minutes/fill-up x 104 trips/year = 3,328 minutes/year, or 55 hours

- 55 hours x $60/hour in labor cost: $3,300
- Actual cost: $3,300 + 165.88 = $3,465.88
- Actual cost minus savings: $3,465.88 - $572.00 = $2,893.88

In the example above, the business owner thought he was being a good steward of his money. He thought he was making the best decision for his business by watching fuel cost, which was a large part of his yearly budget. But the reality was that the decision to try and cut fuel cost ended up costing him an additional $2,893.88 per year (per crew) in additional labor and fuel costs.

What processes and procedures might be holding your business back? What things are you doing today just because you've always done them like that? What areas "don't need to be worried about," or "are good enough"? I challenge you to pull back the curtain to see the opportunities that are being missed. Invest the time and resources in bettering your business with the help of a trusted advisor to help find any holes that you are inadvertently allowing to sink the ship. Open your eyes to what costs, what efficiencies, what breakthroughs in your business can be made just by tweaking what you have been doing (or not doing). Isaiah 43:18–19 tells us to "forget the former things; do not dwell on the past. See, I am doing a new thing! Now it springs up; do you not perceive it?"

CHAPTER 14

KEEPING UP VS. CATCHING UP

I had just reached the halfway point of the Trident Trail Ultra-Run when the mental dialogue started running through my head. This race consisted of a grueling course comprised entirely of sugar sand, sand dunes, and a brutal start time of four p.m. in the middle of July in Florida. Temperatures were in the mid-nineties, and humidity was about the same. Between the sun and the heat radiating off the sand, it felt like I was running in a desert. This course consisted of a 3.3-mile loop with a simple task of just completing the loop within the hour, then lining up again for the start of the next loop at the top of the hour for another 3.3-mile loop. Simple enough in theory. Most of you reading this are probably thinking, "I can walk three miles in an hour—how hard can that be?" You'd be correct. Most people have an average pace of three miles per hour walking on pavement or flat ground. But when you add in the aspect of sugar sand, elevation, heat, and dehydration, you end up with a race with a completion rate of just over 40 percent.

This is where the idea of *keeping up vs. catching up* was born. When you reach a place of physical and mental exertion, it's easy to let your mind wander, let down your guard, ease up on your goals, and start allowing yourself to slip from the original goals you set out to achieve—all to alleviate some of the immediate pain that you are going through. With each loop completed and each mile done, you face a mental choice to either push through or to let up. The decision from the outside looking in is very simple, but the anguish that is felt when you're going through it makes it another story.

The first choice is to *keep up*. Keeping up means pushing through at the original pace that you started at. Running is a good illustration of this. Say you set out to run at a ten-minute-per-mile pace. Then, after each segment—half-mile, mile, or whatever your chosen interval—you can verify that you are keeping up with your agreed-upon pace. This pace is the predetermined goal that you have for the task at hand. In the moment, you may be mentally fighting with yourself to keep this pace, deliberating in your own mind and looking for just a little relief to the current pace to catch your breath or to ease the pain.

So, what's the harm in easing up? What's the harm in slowing the pace, catching your breath, and walking a few short strides? The mind is a beautiful thing. Your mind will undoubtedly start to justify the inevitable consequences. "An eleven-minute mile is fine. I'll still have plenty of time before the next round starts," or, "Everyone around me is walking, so I might as well walk myself," to the extreme of, "Half a race is still more than what my friends and family would do. This is enough."

Keeping Up vs. Catching Up

Whenever we take our focus off the goal—anytime we let our minds wander—we allow two potential outcomes to occur. Sticking with the running example, if we let up on our ten-minute-per-mile pace, then to finish the race within our predetermined goal of ten-minute miles (or thirty-three minutes for the 3.3-mile loop), we will have to run each additional mile after the slowdown at a faster pace.

This is what we refer to as *catch-up*. If we break it down logically, we know that our bodies are already fatigued and we are already having a difficult time keeping up with our current pace. But mentally, we convince ourselves that if we get a little bit of rest—a little bit of relief—things will be easier. The reality of this, though, is it's not true. In running, this means if our pace drops from our ten-minute goal per mile to eleven minutes per mile, then we need to increase our pace for the next two miles to bring ourselves back in line with our original goal by running two 9.5-minute miles. What typically happens when our bodies are already depleted and we then try to push harder and faster than what we originally planned for? We typically blow up. Our heart rate spikes, we overheat, and we end up taxing our bodies even more than if we had stayed the course of our original plan. This then results in additional delays, or worse—complete failure.

In business, this is where your business plan sets the pace. Your business plan is what shows the trajectory to reach the finish line of your race. For most businesses, the finish line is the end of a fiscal year, quarter, or season. Once this plan is set in place, it's simple math to break down what you need to do to stay the course for any month, week, day, hour, shift, or minute, depending on how much tracking you'd like to do.

If we take business X, for instance, that has a goal of $1,200,000 in gross annual sales, then it's easy to break down the pace as follows:

- $1,200,000 Revenue Goal, Year
- $100,000 Revenue Goal, Month
- $23,076 Revenue Goal, Week
- $3,288 Revenue Goal, Day
- $137 Revenue Goal, Hour

Once we know our pace, then we can develop our marketing plan to reach this goal and keep this pace. With our plan in place, we implement our marketing budget and allocate the resources over the course of the year to reach this goal. So, you ask, What happens if we fall behind? If we fall behind, then we end up in catch-up mode. Catch-up mode in business feels a lot like catch-up mode in running. To give us some numbers to work with, let's use the same goals as business X above, but instead, let's assume that January sales were zero dollars, which resulted in the need for catch-up for the remaining eleven months of the year.

- $1,200,000 Revenue Goal, Year
- $109,091 Revenue Goal, Month
- $25,000 Revenue Goal, Week
- $3,593 Revenue Goal, Day
- $150 Revenue Goal, Hour

From the numbers above, we can see that our shortcoming in January resulted in a required increase of about 9 percent for the remaining months. So, the question then becomes, How do we get there? If we put together a realistic business plan for sales that truly estimates what our company is capable of producing during the twelve-month period, have a realistic marketing budget to reach that number, and have a reasonable staff to efficiently and effectively produce or supply the product or service in that period, then what's the outcome?

Keeping up is the baseline of what we can actually accomplish as a realistic goal. When we enter catch-up phase, then we have to reevaluate how to maintain the goal. If we need to increase sales by 9 percent, then it would only make sense that our marketing budget would need to increase by a similar percentage to reach that goal. If our budget and pricing were already set based on our original goal, then increasing our advertising budget—assuming the price of product and service stay the same—would result in a decrease in net profit.

If our staff was able to work efficiently to reach the original goal, then each full-time employee working forty hours per week would need to increase their hours to working 43.6 hours per week, assuming a linear correlation to the increased sales/work needed to stay on task. Or, we would need to hire on 9 percent more workers to keep everyone's workload the same if we don't want to burn out our employees.

Paying overtime or hiring on more staff to reach these catch-up goals will once again cost the business more money. If we can't increase prices, we may, as lots of businesses do to increase sales, reduce prices to bring in more business. The net result once again will be a decrease to the profit of the business.

I have worked with lots of business owners in this position, particularly in the construction industry where the owners put the added burden on themselves to try and make up the difference. They realize they can't increase prices, they don't have the money for increased advertising, and they barely have enough employees as it is, so they take the burden on themselves. By doing this, they devalue themselves. They put zero value on their time and effort and just focus on reaching the goals of the business. They become slaves to the business. They run the extra sales appointments to save paying commissions to reduce the marketing budget. They work the extra hours to not hire additional employees. They do the work that is needed to try and catch up to where they need their business to be to try and right the course.

For those that can keep up the pace and right the ship, it sometimes comes at a cost at home. More time at the office means less time with family. The added stress comes home and can boil over. The lack of balance in life and additional demand from playing catch-up typically turn into a never-ending cycle. As humans, we can only go so hard for so long. It may be a day, a week, a month, a quarter, or a year, but at some point we reach our max.

When playing catch-up, though, like in the race, when you finally do catch up, you don't have the margin to take the pedal off the metal. Once you catch up, you just have to resume your normal pace. For most, this ends up in a teeter-totter effect on their businesses. They will have huge sales one month and fall off drastically the next. Or they will have a great month of success and profitability only to take time off the next month to go on vacation and recharge the batteries, to find themselves playing catch-up once again when they get back to work. Or, they will find themselves stretched too thin, resulting in poor customer service, experience, or quality of products, which then in turn creates lower brand value and once again increases work.

So, how is this avoidable? The magic formula lies in your business plan. Your plan is the roadmap for success in your business. The road map has to contain forecasts for success based on your team's realistic abilities and the resources available. To find this limit, you can pressure test your business when you are operating at an efficient level to see where you can increase and to show the weaknesses in your organization. This allows you to tweak your plan and revise your goals for future periods based off these assessments. But living in the catch-up—living above your means or pushing your team at redline for extended periods—will take its toll on every owner, employee, business, and—most importantly—your family.

The reason we all become entrepreneurs is to take control of our futures and to provide a better way of life for our families and loved ones. Doing this means being a good steward of all things allocated to us. This is not just a financial issue. This is all things in life. Faith, time, love, finance, health, and fitness all need your attention to steward them properly. Stealing from one to satisfy another sometimes is required for a season. But be careful not to fall in the trap of putting one above the other and seeing what you've worked so hard for slip away.

What is the takeaway from all this? As business owners, we spend (or we should spend) a significant amount of time and effort putting together the plan and goals for our businesses. With all the time and effort involved in putting this plan together, it's important that we share it with our team.

Be up front in regard to what everyone is expected to do to keep pace within the company, and share with them the requirements and what will happen if their pace is not met. Be realistic with these goals.

Returning to the running analogy, maybe you can run a five-minute mile. That's great, but can you run twenty-six of them in a row? Your business is a marathon. The pace that you set in your plan needs to be one at which you can start the race and finish the race. If you get halfway through the year and realize you've been able to increase efficiencies, your employees have gotten more productive, you've streamlined processes, and you are crushing goals, then you know where you can increase and revise your goals for next year. Your plan is not static. You can tweak and change it throughout the year. If you find yourself exceeding goals, then maybe it is time to capitalize on these accomplishments to increase profitability for yourself and your team, or to focus some time and attention on some of the other areas in life that may not have been stewarded properly in seasons past.

> Work brings profit, but mere talk leads to poverty! Wealth is a crown for the wise; the effort of fools yields only foolishness. (Proverbs 14:23–24 NLT)

CHAPTER 15

PRACTICE

Effort doesn't guarantee success. It only removes the guarantee of failure.
—Eric Davis

In the age of the search for an easy button, or instant gratification, it seems as though something has been lost. Everyone is created equal by their maker, and we have all been blessed with the same twenty-four hours in our days. With that in mind, the difference between those who do and those who don't really comes down to just one thing. The *Oxford Languages* dictionary defines *effort* as "a vigorous or determined attempt."[1] An attempt. Not success, but simply making the attempt, or putting in effort, can make you successful. In most scenarios, effort is the only thing separating you from what you want. If you are too afraid to try, then what is the certain result? Failure. If you can't even get up to the plate, then you're not even giving yourself a chance. If you don't get out of bed in the morning, you're not even giving yourself a chance at being successful.

---

1. *Oxford Languages*, s.v. "effort (*n.*)," accessed December 15, 2023.

This might hit close to home. You might be reading this, thinking, "Dang, yep that's me." How many times did you hit the snooze? How many ideas have come to your head that you could have done—that you should have done? Are you stuck in a job you don't like? Do you dream of going out and starting a business on your own but your fear or insecurities keep you from even trying? The single most important asset when it comes to building a business is yourself. You are the rock for your business.

> Therefore everyone who hears these words of Mine and puts them into practice is like a wise man who built his house on the rock. The rain came down, the streams rose, and the winds blew and beat against that house; yet it did not fall, because it had its foundation on the rock. (Matthew 7:24–25)

In this Scripture, we see that those who base their principles on the rock that is Jesus stand on the firmest foundation. In your business, when you form your plans and goals based on Him, you are standing on solid ground. Your business and its principles become shaped and formed around your ideals. Knowing that you stand firmly on that rock, you then bring your best toward completing your goals. You can single-handedly control the effort that goes into making this the best business for yourself. Control what you can control. You might not be the smartest—I know I'm not. You might not be the best at sales. You might not have the best idea, but the one thing you can control is the effort you put into the business. Where you fall short, you can overcome with effort. If you are not the most efficient, then work harder. If something takes you longer, put in more hours. If you're not the best at sales, then go on more sales calls. You can control the amount of effort that you put into your business. This effort is directly related to the success that will come from what you do. As the great Alexander Graham Bell once said, "The only difference between success and failure is the ability to take action."

Additionally, effort increases ability. You know what happens when you go on more sales calls than your competition? You end up getting better at what you were previously not good at, and you end up making more sales. What happens when you get better at something that you're not good at? Your efficiency improves. You know what happens then? Your closing percentages increase, and your business grows. You just outworked the better salesperson and became a better salesperson yourself. The repetition, putting in the work, and putting in the time are what it takes. This is what you can control. This is the aspect that will give you the results that you want.

Business owners today think that they can sit around and post something online or build a website and people will flock to them. You have to get out of the mindset that you or your business will become something if you're not willing to do something. The doing is the separator. The effort is the difference. The hard work is what separates those that do from those that talk about doing. Many people want to be something. It could be argued that everyone wants to be something. The reality, though, is that only a small percentage are willing to do what is necessary and put in the work to get there.

Those times when you get up early and you work hard, those times when you stay up late and you work hard, those times when you don't feel like working—you're too tired, you don't want to push yourself—but you do it anyway. That is actually the dream. That's the dream. (Kobe Bryant)[2]

So, what do you want to do? Do you want to guarantee your failure? Not trying is already failing. Read that again. Yes, most people think that if you don't start something, then you can't fail. I think of it the opposite way. If you don't start something, you've already failed. Any missed opportunity that you wanted in life where you were too afraid to take the shot, to try, or to do anything about it is a fail. Put it in the L column—it's a *loss*. You failed without even stepping on the court. You wanted something but decided you're too much of a loser to even get in the game.

It's all about effort. It's trying. It's trying and trying again. Once you are trying, then you aren't failing. If Kobe missed a shot in a game, did he fail? No, he didn't fail—he missed a shot, and he was going to take another shot and another until he made one and then another and another. Trying and not coming up with the desired result is not failing. You could start a business and put in work and realize that there is no market for the product you are trying to create. That's not an L. That's putting in the effort to get you to your goal. That's getting in experience, getting education, and putting in the time to hone your craft.

Let's set the record straight. Life isn't about making things easy. It's not about taking the easiest path. It's not about what

---

2. Karen Mizoguchi, "Kobe Bryant's Life and Legacy," *People*, January 26, 2022, Kobe Bryant's Jersey Retirement Ceremony Speech, December 18, 2017, people.com/sports/kobe-bryant-mamba-mentality-quotes-to-live-by.

you can do to make your day more comfortable. It's about being comfortable with being uncomfortable. It's about being okay and excelling when things get tough—when your back is against the wall, when things are hard, when you are looking down the barrel at a difficult task. Life is about having the mindset that you put in the work, all the hard work you put in will breed success, and the effort—the possibility of being uncomfortable—doesn't stand in the way of your success. The only thing uncomfortable to you becomes not accomplishing the task at hand. When the uncomfortable becomes your comfort zone, then you know that you have the fortitude to push past any obstacle.

When you overcome complacency and say, "That's not the life for me. That has no place in my business," then you mentally set yourself up for the win. You program your mind such that whatever uncomfortable situation your find yourself in, it will be way less difficult than taking the L that will surely come if you run from the situation. You see, that's the thing about uncomfortable situations. They don't just go away. You can hold them off—you can even run from them for a while. You can dodge, you can weave, and you can avoid them. But at some point, you are going to have to face them. You will either face the uncomfortable and overcome it, coming out stronger on the other side, or you will be consumed by it and be spit out the backside of it in a worse place than where you started. The choice is yours. The only easy task is the task that's already done. Once completed, you can say whether or not something was easy. The harder you work, the easier the hard stuff will be. But life will never be easy. To improve, to press forward, to thrive, you need to be able to thrive in the uncomfortable. You will do what others won't, you will excel where others can't, and you will make what others view as impossible look easy.

> Let us not become weary in doing good, for at the proper time we will reap a harvest if we do not give up. (Galatians 6:9)

CHAPTER 16

SELF-MADE

I have to start this chapter with the warning that you might not like what you read here. If you like to make excuses that it's someone else's fault that you're in the situation you're in—if you blame anything that has happened in your life on your parents, siblings, teachers, or society, then you might just want to skip to chapter 17 now.

If you decided to keep reading, then this chapter will help you. To save typing, I have to be blunt and not draw this point out. I am writing very directly, so I thank you for continuing to read. You might not like it, you might get mad about it, and you might think I could have said things in a better, nicer, kinder way, but at the end of the day, life's too short for all that. I love you, and I want to hammer this point home. And the only way I can do that is by being direct.

My favorite quote is, "Everyone in the world is self-made; but only the successful take credit for it." When I read this, it has me coming back to it, reading it over and over again. At first, I tried to shoot holes in it, thinking, "Nay, not really," but the reality is that it's the truest statement that I've heard. Everyone in the world—every single one of us—is self-made.

Think of that—you, me, your mom, dad, neighbor, sister, brother, cousin—everyone you meet is self-made. We all wake up every day with the same twenty-four hours to get out there and to do our thing. What we do with those hours is what sets us all apart from one another. The humbling aspect of this is that we all need to take credit for being self-made. You are self-made. I am self-made. Every one of us is the sum of all of our decisions up to this point in time.

In life, God created us all equal, in His image. So, as Christians, it is our responsibility to live up to this image in which God created us. Think about that. How we display our own image is a reflection of how we represent the image of God. If He created us in His image, then it's our duty to uphold this standard in our own lives so that others will look to us and see the image of God.

Wow. That's a little deep. But it's true. Pastor Jeremy Dunn says, "If you read your Bible, it'll talk to you." So, when we read the Word of God, we have to realize the meaning of the words we read. If we can accept that we are all made by God in His image, then it's only reasonable to think that we should all display God's image in how we work, what we do, what we say, and how we live. If we frame all of our challenges, decisions, and choices in life with this question in mind—"Is what I am doing living up to the image of God?"—then we have a clear path in regard to what we should be doing or how we can improve the choices we make on a daily basis to reflect God's image.

In the day to day, these life choices become our habits. These habits can be good or bad. They can create gains or losses. They can display the image of God in us, or not. These habits are what transform us as human beings and enable the decisions that we have made in the past to become firmer habits in the present and the future. I'm not saying that a bad habit can't be changed, but one must ask the question of how or why the bad habit formed in the first place.

We all have the ability to make good or bad choices each and every day. Each day, we are bombarded with information. Ever answer to every question is at our fingertips. One would think that with this increase in access to knowledge, we would all be smarter. If we look around, it doesn't appear that's the case. So, although we know how to get the answers to the questions that we have (e.g., about fitness, nutrition, financial education, or morality), we may or may not choose to research them. Or, if we do know what to do, we may just simply choose not to do it for the sake of convenience. This is where we all show that we are self-made.

You're either in the gym becoming self-made, or you are sitting on the couch becoming self-made. Both people have the same choice to make. One is self-made fit, and one is self-made fat. This isn't anyone else's decision but yours. Any excuse you come up with is just that. An excuse. Any reason for not liking something in your life but not being willing to do something different to change it is laziness. Excuses and laziness are what create the self-made reality that many of you live in.

Your finances are in the dumps? What have you done to educate yourself? Your finances are self-made. It's your responsibility to become the best at each and every life skill to hone your craft. You have the duty to your family, your kids, your community, and your church to do your best to live your life the right way.

So, why do you allow yourself to fall into bad habits? God has given you free will. He will bless you and guide you, but at the end of the day, He will not make you do anything. He will nudge you, He will remind you, and He will put people in your life that you can lean on, but He is not going to snatch you off the couch or create a six-pack on your belly out of the remnants of Cheetos dust. Change will require you to make the decision for the version of self-made that you want in your life. Some of your choices are conscious, and some are unconscious. The more bad choices you make and the more your choices become unconscious, the harder they will be for you to overcome.

The journey to being self-made is long. This started for all of us as kids, transformed as we became teens, marinated us in our twenties, and became embedded in us in our thirties. No one intentionally thinks, "I have two choices—one is good for me one is bad. Which one do I choose?" No, you make the wrong choice once, and then you just don't ask the question of yourself the next day. You don't repeatedly make the same mistake—you just allow the mistake to become a habit in your life. It becomes an automatic decision—one that takes no effort and no thought. Once it becomes a habit, it becomes a norm. No longer does a bad decision give you guilt, because it is the new norm. Once it's a norm, then it becomes an acceptable thing in your life that you don't have to think about or make a decision on. You get to turn on the autopilot.

Then, to double down on this, you find friends that have the same interest as you. So now, Joe and Tom (let's call them) will come over and sit on the couch and eat snacks and drink soda with you. This "norm" gets engrained deeper and deeper. Why would you even think about doing something else? Joe and Tom are your friends—you like hanging with them. They like snacks and soda. You think to yourself, "I can't ask them to go to the gym—they aren't going to want to do that." So instead, you sit on the couch, eating ice cream and lapping syrup out of your belly button every night. You have no better reason to do it than that you did it last night and the night before that, and soon it becomes what you look forward to doing. You worked hard today playing your video games and holding down your mom's basement, so you deserve to eat ice cream. This becomes your norm. It becomes a reward for the life that you created. You're a self-made couch-sitting ice-cream-eating Netflix-binging all-star.

But all things have a *but*. Just like you fell into this rut, you can also break these habits and establish new boundaries for your life that will allow you to become the self-made person that you truly want to be. We are all created equal, remember. We are all given the same twenty-four hours in a day. The difference just comes down to how you use the six inches between your ears. Do you turn your brain off and go into ice cream land, or do you keep it on, engaged, and asking yourself questions about how you can make your own life and the lives around you better?

Activity breeds activity. If you surround yourself with a bunch of ice-cream-eating, TV-watching, couch-lounging people, then you're going to more than likely fall into that category yourself. Surround yourself with fit, high-energy, active, successful people, and guess what. You are going to become who you surround yourself with. But—once again, the *but*. These groups take effort to get into. If you are a super-fit, high-energy, in-shape, healthy-eating individual, then more than likely you're not going to want the ice cream crew to join your team. Similarly, the fit, in-shape, healthy person isn't going to want you to join their crew if you can't roll yourself off the couch.

So, it all comes down to you at this point. Turn your brain back on. Look at your life. Look at what you are doing to self-sabotage your self-made story and start running each decision through your head. To provide a point of reference, a normal day as a high-producing adult should go something like this:

Your alarm goes off. Do you hit snooze and roll over, or kick the sheets off and get out of bed?

Now that you're up, what do you do? Eat a jelly donut? Or drink some water and take a morning walk, do pushups, sit-ups, or something else?

Now that you're done working out, do you eat some Fruity Pebbles or an adult breakfast with some fruit, a protein shake, some eggs, or something similar?

Great. Now that you're fed with some actual nutrition, do you fall back on the couch in your underwear to watch some cartoons, or do you hop in the shower to take on the day?

Great decision—you're showered up. Now, put on some clothes so you look semi-presentable and get out of the house. This means iron your shirt, put on some clean shoes, and shave (guys and girls).

Now you're out of the house, and you've already had a couple of wins. You're up, you didn't hit snooze, you put in some work, you ate some breakfast, and you're at the job.

You see Pete at the water cooler. Do you go up to Pete and talk about the game last night? No, you stiff-arm Pete on your way to your office for wasting your dang time for the last two years talking about the Cowboys (or insert any other pro-college—or heaven forbid, high school game here. If you are still talking about your high school game and you are not in high school, then there are issues at hand that reading this book will not help). Hint: No one in the real world cares if you know who won. The Cowboys don't care if you watched the game. Your checkbook, your promotion, your company, your business, and your self-made story don't care.

So now, you are working. Are you really working? Are you really putting in effort? Are you making the calls? Are you building your brand? Are you building your business or bettering your team? If you're not, this is where you need a mindset shift. Everything you need to do you need to do as if you're giving glory to God. First Corinthians 10:31 (NLT) tells us, "So whether you eat or drink, or whatever you do, do it all for the glory of God." Are you actually putting in the effort to make a difference? Are you actually putting in the effort like you are trying to bring glory to God's kingdom? Are you grinding it out, giving it 100 percent so you can walk away at the end of the day saying, "I did that. I truly gave it my all"? Or are you hiding at work, hoping no one sees you playing video games and watching YouTube?

Yes, I know you. In my business, I monitored the Wi-Fi at our office to see who was streaming Telemundo and who was putting in work. You do you, but I know when you run these decisions through your head after all the wins you put in this morning, the new you is going to be putting in the work. You're now closing sales, jamming out TPS reports, and conquering the day. Now, bring on lunch.

So, are you going to go to lunch with Pete? Heck no is the answer. You didn't even need to think about it because you're going to the gym at lunch, and you're going to hop on the elliptical during your lunch break to hopefully see some hot honeys. (Yep, you see how your mindset just got tweaked? You developed a little swag in your voice, and your day is transitioning for the better. You have some confidence because you've been winning all morning and you love the way you feel.) Well, thirty minutes at the gym and a quick bite to eat, and you're back at work. That wasn't so difficult, was it?

Now it's afternoon. Pete's going for a pick-me-up. Are you going with him? "Sorry, Pete, I'm on a roll today, my friend." No, you just drop-kicked the door shut and told him to get out of your face. You don't need a pick-me-up. You just worked out twice, had a good breakfast and a great lunch, almost had the nerve to talk to a pretty girl at the gym, closed some deals this morning, and you're going to keep stacking W's.

Four p.m. rolls around. "I'm leaving early, Pete. See you tomorrow, man." Pete asks, "You watching the game tonight?" "Heck no," you respond. "I got stuff to do." "Then what are you going to do tonight?" you ask yourself. "Well, self," you say, "tonight we are going to google how my chubby butt can lose some weight." When you head down this rabbit hole, you realize that meal prepping is a great idea, so you go grocery shopping at the local Piggly Wiggly, you buy a bunch of foods, and you cook them up. You now have food for the rest of the week, and you can eat like a man vs. like a child.

Eight p.m. rolls around. "So, now what am I going to do?" You have already had the most productive day that you've had in a long time. You can easily say, "Lets watch the game. I deserve it. I've been working hard for almost one whole day." But no, you realize you still have more W's out there that you can track down. So, you realize that now that you're a grown up and go grocery shopping, you are saving money vs. ordering all this Uber Eats junk food to your mom's basement. "So, what am I going to do with this extra money?" you think. A quick google search and what do you find? "Roth IRA—wow, that sounds like something I probably should be doing. Well heck," you think. "I'll put the X dollars per month from the money I'm now saving on meal prepping into this. Man, another good idea, and it only took me sixty minutes to set it up and link to my checking account. Today was a good day. I'm beat. Time to go to bed."

That's how you stack W's. This is how you create good habits. This is how you end up moving out of your mom's basement into a place of your own. This is how you become the self-made you that you want to be. Stay focused, stay alert, ask yourself questions. "How is this going to better my life? How is this going to make me a better person? How is this going to better those around me?" If it will better you, do it. If it won't, then don't do it.

You might find that your life is surrounded by Petes. Eliminate the Petes from your life. In your personal life, Petes will hold you back. In your business life, Petes will hold your company back. Petes do not create value; they take up space. If you love Pete, then have a heart-to-heart with him or her. Let him know your goals, let him know your plan, and let him know that it's not about him—this is about you bettering you and becoming the self-made version of yourself that you want to be.

Don't fall into the Pete trap. He will try to hold on to you—the old ways, the lazy ways, and the way you used to be. If that Pete rears his head, you've got to stiff-arm him. In the Bible, Proverbs 27:17 says, "As iron sharpens iron, so one person sharpens another." You can't sharpen iron on something that is soft. To get hard—to better yourself—you have to surround yourself with others that will help you better yourself and hold you to the new standard that you are setting for yourself. You can't sharpen iron with cheese or some other soft, squishy substance. So, surround yourself with those that are putting in the effort and doing, or trying to do, what you want to do and going where you want to be.

If where you want to be is on the couch, I wish you the best. If you don't want that, set your standards high. No one will do it for you. If you feel the true meaning of life is video games and your mom's basement, then you do you. For the rest of you that read this and realize you want more out of your lives, then this is the way to get there.

CHAPTER 17

NEWTON'S LAW

Newton law of inertia states that "an object at rest stays at rest, and an object in motion stays in motion with the same speed and in the same direction unless acted upon by an unbalanced force." The same can be said in business. There are many businesses over the course of history that gained momentum and almost looked unstoppable until some force slowed them down or brought them to a stop.

The first one that comes to mind is Blockbuster Movies. I just turned forty-three years old, so to paint the picture, I'll give a perspective that most of you around my age will probably relate to. Blockbuster was the best date-night activity for anyone—the experience of going with your date to dinner and then stopping by Blockbuster on the way back to your place or hers to pick out a movie together. You can't explain it, but you knew what kind of night it was going to be based on the movie that you picked. Comedy meant it's going to be a fun night. Sad means she's going to cry and snuggle in your arms. Romance.

But besides all this, Blockbuster had the market cornered on the movie-rental business—until they were approached by a wee little startup company called Netflix. Netflix offered to sell to Blockbuster. See, their intentions were not to replace the video-rental model but to improve and expand it. But (there is that word again), Blockbuster didn't want anything to do with them. So, what happened was that Netflix rolled out their own business plan, and the forces of nature brought a screeching halt to Blockbuster's quasi monopoly on the movie-rental business.

Why do I bring this up? The point of all this is that just because something is working, has worked, and did work doesn't mean that it always will or that it won't take massaging, effort, or change to keep the ball rolling. In business, you have an endless number of forces that act against you. You operate in a free market with open competition to your business. Customers have a variety of companies, products, and services to choose from when making their decisions. What makes you stand out? What makes you the one they pick? What keeps your head above water when the market turns, or innovation comes?

To sum it up in one word, Blockbuster's problem was *complacency*. According to *Oxford Languages*, *complacency* is "a feeling of smug or uncritical satisfaction with oneself or one's achievements."[1] The Bible says in Proverbs 1:32: "For the waywardness of the simple will kill them, and the complacency of fools will destroy them." Complacency in business comes in many forms, but the most deadly threat that I have seen is complacency about change. Businesses need to stay relevant,

---

1. *Oxford Languages*, s.v. "complacency (n.)," accessed December 15, 2023.

able to adapt, and able to focus on the now and not on the successes of the past.

Keep your eyes open to market threats and opportunities so when Netflix approaches you as Blockbuster, you entertain it with open eyes, seeing that the world might be changing, that people might rather sit at home and order a movie from their TV without the need to "be kind, rewind," that late fees might become a thing of the past, and that new releases being sold out might no longer be a thing—that you may no longer need to worry about whether the person before you scratched the DVD that you rented and now you are going to miss a part of your favorite movie. All these things could turn your industry upside down, and the house of cards of your empire could come crashing down. (A side note is that Blockbuster had the opportunity to buy Netflix for $50,000,000, but they laughed the Netflix founders out of the room. Today, Netflix is worth an estimated $196.37 billon.)

So, how do you stay motivated and avoid complacency? This complacency can give you a false vision of what is going on. It can cloud your judgement. It can cloud your decisions. It can give you false hopes or a sense of grandeur that failure "won't happen to me" because of your previous success. This is where you need to heed the warning. This is the red, flashing light that screams *Warning!*

If you find yourself in this situation or are blessed to have others around you that will bring this to your attention, then heed the warnings. Just because it worked in the past doesn't mean it will work tomorrow. Just because the pet rock sold one million units doesn't mean you can sell one million units today. Change is inevitable, and effort is required. The Bible discusses humility again and again.

- Romans 12:16 (NLT): "Live in harmony with each other. Don't be too proud to enjoy the company of ordinary people. And don't think you know it all!"
- Proverbs 15:33 (NLT): "Fear of the LORD teaches wisdom; humility precedes honor."
- Psalms 25:9 (NLT): "He leads the humble in doing right, teaching them his way."

A great quote by Benjamin P. Hardy says that "if you have something to brag about, someone will do it for you." If you stay grounded, remember what got you where you are, and don't let success go to your head. If you are always looking to better yourself, your businesses, and those around you, then you can maintain the momentum.

CHAPTER 18

FEEDING THE EGO

Why do we do the things we do? As entrepreneurs, why do we set the goals for ourselves that we set? In my years of coaching and consulting, every time I have sat down to discuss a business, the first thing that has come up is sales revenue. Like a shiny new trophy, sales revenue is the barometer that's shouts to the world, "Look at me, I made it." Sure, sales are an important part of business. Sales are in actuality the lifeblood of business and, for argument's sake, the most important part of the business. Without sales, the business ceases to operate. Without bringing in new revenue, the company no longer has cash to operate. Employees have nothing to do if new sales for products, services, etc., are not made.

But what kind of sales is your business making? I've met with countless entrepreneurs who have filled me with information about how they are going to double, triple, quintuple, or even increase times ten their revenue this year to become a five-, ten-, twenty-five-, or hundred-million-dollar company. My simple response is, Why? Why do you need to hit this revenue number? This question is usually met with confusion. "What do you mean why? It's incredible to grow five times, ten times, or fifty times whatever number." I agree it is. But why do you need to hit this number?

This is the question that will help me understand more about your business than any other question. This is the true driving factor—the true *why* of your business. This is what motivates the decision-makers of your company. You, as the owner—what are you focused on as the barometer of your business? The typical business owner after a pause goes into some spiel about how larger growth will allow the company greater sustainability, market economic resilience, and lower cost due to economy of scale. All of these are admirable goals, but once again, Why?

This is typically when a slight irritation sets in, and the tone and mood of the conversation may slightly change. "What do you mean why? Greater sustainability, market resilience, and scaling our operations are good things!" I once again agree. My question simply is, *Why* do you need to increase revenue to accomplish those goals? If these are truly the goals of the company, then simply increasing revenue isn't the easiest way or even the most efficient way of getting there.

This is when things usually unravel, and true answers start to come out. "Five years ago, we did one million dollars in sales and broke even. Then we doubled revenue and were able to churn out a small profit in year two. Year three, we doubled again and churned a 5 percent profit on just under five million dollars. Year four, we did $7,500,000 and dialed in our margins around 20 percent, and this year we should hit. At ten-million-dollar revenue, we were operating at 20 percent net profit. If we can get to twenty million dollars, I'm confident that we will still be able to maintain a 15 percent net profit."

This is where the answer is finally revealed. The *why* isn't economy of scale; the *why* isn't market economic resilience; the *why* isn't lower costs due to economy of scale. The *why* is bottom-line profit. Profit is the true *why*.

The true goal is masked. The *why* is hidden in the ego of business. No entrepreneur wants to see their revenue number go down. This is their bragging point. This is their show-off number. This is the number that Wall Street talks about. Apple is a three-trillion-dollar company.

But in the real world, in real life, the *why* has to be considered. Why chase the dollar, as in the example above, to do more work to earn less net profit per dollar worked? You're working harder, doing more, and in return putting less value on the dollars that you are producing, for the sole goal of producing more of them. This is where the expression "Revenue feeds the ego, profit feeds your family" comes in. Sure, I'd love to have a three-trillion-dollar company like Apple, but not at the cost of sacrificing my family for profit. Let's break down the goals of one entrepreneur's particular business to see if increasing revenue will truly accomplish the goals they are setting out for, or if increasing profit would better accomplish these goals.

Greater Sustainability

Let's take the example above and grow this company from a ten-million-dollar-per-year-in-revenue company to a twenty-million-dollar-per-year company. The first stated goal of the business owner is "sustainability." With the growth of the company revenue, it's safe to assume that they will have to hire on (increase) sales personnel to generate sales and increase facility size, expenses, marketing budget, production department, admin department to help support the sales, customer service, etc.

With all this growth, they are already assuming lower profitability for their company, plus the potential doubling of their operations. If the economy slumps, if their product falls out of favor, if governmental guidelines change for their product or service, or if more competition enters the market, driving the pricing lower, then it's safe to assume that the pressure on their bottom line will suffer even more. Since they've already cut estimated profit by 25 percent (20 percent to 15 percent), then what is the net sum of the financials if they end up 25 percent lower on the revenue projections as well and their estimated profit is 25 percent less than what they thought it would take to get that revenue (11.25 percent vs. 15 percent estimated)?

When I come in to do a year-end review of their business, if they are focused on the revenue, they will once again sit down and discuss how they had another incredible year of growth. They increased sales 50 percent and were able to increase "greater sustainability and market share." If I didn't care about them and their families, I'd pat them on the back and send them on their way, saying that they had the magic formula for their business, and it sounded like they had everything under control.

In reality, they may. From my stance, though, they don't. In business finance as well as personal finance, I feel as though we have the responsibility to steward each and every dollar with the greatest ability and efficiency that we possibly can. If there are inefficiencies, if there is waste, and if there isn't the utmost care taken with each and every dollar entrusted to us, then we have taken our eye off the ball.

As we break down this company's year-end review, we look at what they did:

- $15,000,000 Revenue (50% gain YOY)
- $1,687,500 Net Profit (-43.75% loss YOY) (11.25% actual vs. 20% net profit of previous year)

In this example, the company set out with the goal to increase sustainability for their business. Now they have created a business with higher expenses, larger monthly burn, and less net profit for the owners. In this example, the supposed goal of growing revenue to increase sustainability has created the opposite effect. They now have less net profit to depend on in a downturn, they have less net profit to distribute to owners, and they have less net profit to bonus employees. Their organization is working harder, not smarter. They are working harder for less profit than when they were doing 33 percent less revenue. Once again, the question is why. Oh—market resilience was the second reason for their top-end growth.

Market Economic Resilience

Let us break down this company's market resilience with the increased revenue number. Sticking with the numbers in the example above, we will assume that they hit the fifteen million dollars in revenue, giving them the desired 50 percent YOY growth in revenue. With this, the premise is that by being a larger player in the market, they will be able to improve market "economic resilience." First, let's take a look at what economic resilience is, courtesy of EDA.gov. Economic resilience is the "ability to prepare a region to anticipate, withstand, and bounce back from any type of shock, disruption, or stress it may experience."[1]

Now we have to ask the question of whether this company's desired goal of market resilience was met based on the increase in revenue. How is the company more resilient? This answer can be opinion based. They as the entrepreneurs can answer this based on whatever criteria they feel have added resilience to their business from this increase in revenue. What factors have improved the company's resilience? What factors with this increase in revenue have improved the ability of the company to withstand a downturn?

Great. We have all the positives that the increased revenue has added to their market resilience. Let's continue to run the scenario through a few more questions to find out if they have added resilience or exposed some vulnerabilities.

- Has gross profit gone up or down?
- Have staff efficiencies gone up or down?
- Has owner benefit improved?
- Has product quality improved?
- Has customer experience improved?
- Has employee satisfaction improved?

Once we answer all these questions, let's rehash where the business falls. Has it increased its market resilience? Using

---

1. "Economic Resilience," U.S. Economic Development Administration, eda.gov/resources/comprehensive-economic-development-strategy/content/economic-resilience/, accessed December 18, 2023.

the data we have from the examples above, we know that profit has gone down and owner benefit has not improved. We don't have enough info to know if customer experience has changed or if employee satisfaction has improved. I would read into this example and assume the product quality has not improved due to the decrease in profit. If the product had improved in quality, I would assume profit had maintained or increased the quality. Better-quality products typically equal higher price, higher value, and higher cost.

My overall summary of the sample business would be that increasing revenue has not improved their market resilience. The simple aspect of selling more did not improve any of what I consider important KPI's (key performance indicators) to truly say that this company's market resilience improved.

Lower Cost and Economy of Scale

When they speak of economies of scale, what is their actual goal? They are looking to reduce their acquisition cost of product, service, material, transaction fee, shipping, etc., based on the sheer volume at which they are producing for vendor, supplier, subcontractor, etc. If they are trying to reduce their overall cost of product or cost of goods sold, then what is the underlying driver? If they are happy with their profit margin, happy with their company structure, and happy with all things, then once again we ask, Why? What are their goals in lowering their cost of goods sold, and why are those goals important to their business?

Using the example above of growing revenue 50 percent (YOY), what economies of scale did this provide to their business? What level of revenue do they need to reach the goal that they are striving toward for their business? If we look at the net results for the business above, then what do we see? Sales did increase 50 percent (YOY), but profit decreased 43.75 percent. So, if their summary of the business is correct and their business did in fact improve economy of scale and reduce its cost of goods sold, then the issues are far worse than they appear. The numbers above show a 43.75 percent drop in net profit, and this includes the economies of scale the business has been able to take advantage of and implement over the last year. The question then becomes, Where would their numbers be if they had not been able to take advantage of these economies of scale with their business? What would happen if they lose these economies of scales in future years—where do profits go then? Can they keep up the increased sales numbers if cost of goods rises, or was this what allowed them to increase sales by 50 percent? Once your business has adjusted its numbers, its staff, its margin, etc., to take advantage of the benefits that the additional size of the organization has created, then the loss of such benefit or change in benefit can have a devastating effect on the bottom line.

Once again, when we lay this out, we come back to the original question: Why? Why do we need increased revenue? This whole exercise is to open up the mind and reset the thinking to see that the question isn't "How big can I get to reach my goals?" The question is "How do I reach a highly efficient organization that maximizes profit?" Remember, profit feeds the family. Revenue feeds the ego.

As entrepreneurs, your time is valuable. Maximizing and improving efficiencies in your organization is the goal to truly reach your *why*. In all of the three examples above, the end result was that the entrepreneurs' true goal of increasing revenue was to increase profit. But with all three changes that were made and with all the goals that were set, the end result was a negative effect on the goal they were aiming for. The desired outcome could not be reached based on the goals set and the processes set in place. Revenue grew 50 percent, staff increased, economies of scale were achieved. From the outside looking in, the goals of the business were successful and the owners sitting around summarizing their business plan were high-fiving each other for a job well done. In reality, they exposed their company to potential threats and higher risk from downturn than they would have had they maintained the original revenue and profit guidance from the previous year.

All growth is not the same growth for growth's sake. Growth without the proper goal for growth can stretch your organization and expose weakness that is avoidable if you ask the real questions to find out what the true goals are when you say you want to grow. "Take delight in the LORD,…trust in Him and He will do this: He will make your righteous reward shine like the dawn, your vindication like the noonday sun" (Psalm 37:4–6).

CHAPTER 19

CLOSING THOUGHTS

As entrepreneurs, we all fundamentally want one thing. We have all taken into our own hands the responsibility for our lives and those of our families, employees, and investors because we truly believe that we can improve upon or create something in a way that has never been done before. With that, we take on an immense amount of stress and sign up for long nights, hard work, and doing what others are unwilling to do or simply can't do.

But with that also comes the desire for happiness and fulfillment. We want to provide for our families, we want to provide for our staff, and we want to build better, happier lives for ourselves. This can come in many shapes or forms. Everyone's happiness, or fulfillment, quotient is different. For some, it is all about time. For some, it's financial independence. For some, it's creative freedom. For some, it's wealth. For some, it's legacy. For some, it's even fear that drives them to wake up every day and hustle.

But whatever your reason is, I want you to take a step back and look at where you are, where you came from, and what you have accomplished on this road. No matter what your aspirations are, or where you want your business to go, pause and see if where you are is still aligned with the original dream that you set out to achieve. Are you creating this business to increase happiness in your life and your family, for example? Then this goal should be the underpinning of every decision that you make. Will the decision you make today improve your happiness or your family's well-being? Simple in theory—maybe harder in reality. When this is the underlying criterion for all the decisions you make, then you will make the decisions that will bring together your work with your home.

Happiness is the sum of what you think, say, and do. Simply put, if you align your values with the decisions that you make and with the goals of your life, you will achieve happiness and fulfillment in the end. To do this, you have to stack your priorities correctly. If you switch the order of your priorities, things will become unaligned. If you put one in front of the other, then you will not reach the end goal.

> Seek first His kingdom and His righteousness, and all these things will be given to you as well. (Matthew 6:33)

Jesus tells us that if we seek first His kingdom and righteousness, then all the other things we need will be added to it. Let this be your north star to guide you through all your business and personal pursuits. God is at the top of your hierarchy of priorities. Finances are at the bottom of the hierarchy. If you seek Him first, you will find that in addition to receiving citizenship in His spiritual kingdom and His righteousness to take the place of your unrighteousness, you will also have all your other needs met—whether those are family, fitness, or financial needs. With your faith as your guiding principle, everything else in your life lines up. Only by aligning your priorities and your goals will you truly reach the level of fulfillment you set out to achieve.

Faith
Family
Fitness
Finance

= Fulfillment

ABOUT THE AUTHOR

Robert M. Donovan is a seasoned serial entrepreneur, former investment advisor, and financial coach who has over twenty-five years of extensive experience in the financial world. Armed with his passion for building wealth and his commitment to helping everyday people become masters of their finances, Robert loves to empower his readers by providing them with the key tools and insights they need to make smart monetary choices, plan for retirement, and achieve financial freedom.

Having built a successful business that he sold to a Fortune 500 company, Robert's unique mix of business expertise and his religious outlook has inspired him to share his story with his readers. He aims to blend tried-and-tested advice with biblical principles that will help guide anyone to a life of financial success. Robert earned his MBA in Advanced Finance from the University of South Florida. For additional tools, teachings, and resources visit: DonovanDevelopment.com.

www.ingramcontent.com/pod-product-compliance
Lightning Source LLC
Chambersburg PA
CBHW050906160426
43194CB00011B/2313